PEACE

MY FINAL GIFT

Mary L. Cardin

About the Author

Mary Cardin is the owner of Shining Star Caregivers, an in-home non-medical senior care giving service. She currently lives and works in Durango, Colorado. Mary is dedicated to continuing the legacy of her late husband's artwork. His paintings can be viewed on the Chris Cardin website at

www.clcardin.com

marycardin@gmail.com

Mary L. Cardin

First Edition, 2012

Printed in USA

ISBN-13: 978-0615342986

To Christopher Lyle

As long as I live, you will live.

Many of the names within this text have been changed to protect the privacy of the individuals involved.

Editing and writing support services
provided by

Strength of Spirit
Consulting and Writing Services

www.strengthofspiritconsulting.com
sandra@strengthofspiritconsulting.com

Back cover photography by

Allison Ragsdale Photography
Durango, Colorado

www.allisonragsdalephotography.com
allison@allisonragsdalephotography.com

Mary L. Cardin

Contents

Mary L. Cardin

<u>Chapter One</u>

Awakened

The phone rang, startling me awake. It was
Wednesday night after Labor Day in 2007. Who would be
calling me so close to midnight? I picked up the phone and
looked at the number that had registered on my caller ID.
Area code 505. New Mexico. Who do I know in New
Mexico?

The caller identified himself as officer Dom
Gallegos with the New Mexico State Police. He asked if I
was Mary Cardin. When I told him I was, he wanted to
know if I knew a Christopher Lyle Cardin.

"Yes, of course. He's my husband."

The officer informed me that a black Chevy Avalanche with Pennsylvania license plates had been found at the Rio Grande Gorge Bridge in Taos, New Mexico. The vehicle had reportedly been parked at the bridge for two days, unattended. The officer asked if this was Chris' truck. I told him that it was. The officer continued his questioning.

"No one has reportedly seen Chris for those two days. Do you know where he is?"

"No, I don't. I haven't seen him for several months."

According to Officer Gallegos, Chris was now considered to be a missing person, since his truck was apparently abandoned at the bridge. He asked me if I thought suicide could be a possibility. I hesitated, my mind whirling with the nature of his question. And I was just beginning to come out of that confused, unclear fuzziness that lingered from being jostled out of a deep sleep. It was all too much to handle, especially at that time of night. It took a while for me to respond. I finally said,

"Yes, suicide is a possibility."

Chris had talked about suicide in the past. He first told me about his attempt and his feelings of wanting to die before we were married, during a trip back to Arkansas to visit his mom and step-father. When he was in his early twenties, Chris had plowed his brand new, red Dodge Challenger into a tree. Miraculously, he had not been injured and walked away from the so-called accident.

Chris had just called me six days ago. He couldn't have. Those thoughts ran through me over and over and over. He just called me six days ago. He couldn't have. He just called me. Six days ago.

———————————————

I had been rattling a shopping cart up and down the aisles of Durango's South City Market when I got Chris' call. It was right around 5 p.m. and the store was busy. I was perusing the cereal aisle when my cell phone rang. It was the first time Chris had contacted me since our separation in May, nearly three and a half months earlier. Just the sound of his voice broke me into a million pieces all over again. A picture in my mind of the last time I saw him shook me. I told him I couldn't talk to him now. Not like this in a grocery store, for heavens sake. Not in public. It was just too hard.

Chris understood. After all our years together, Chris did understand me well. He read my body movements and he could hear what my heart felt in my voice over the phone.

"You haven't heard my voice in a long while. Will you call me back when you're done shopping?"

I promised I would. The tears kept coming as I mindlessly threw who knows what into my cart, aisle after aisle. Earlier, when I first walked into the store, my world was different. I planned to choose some special treats for my sweet niece, Nellie, who was flying in the next day to spend the Labor Day weekend with me. Nellie always preferred healthy food choices, so I wanted to have plenty of fresh fruit and yogurt in the house—all of her favorites. But at that moment, food seemed unimportant. Why now? My heart had longed to hear from Chris every day since we separated. He had finally called. Why now?

The time I spent to finish shopping, standing in the checkout line and paying the cashier was just long enough to collect myself and my emotions. I watched my fingers shake as I dialed Chris' cell number. I suspected he hadn't called me before now because it was his only way of dealing with the emotional pain of our separation. I guessed that he had to block out that part of his life in order to be able to handle it and survive.

Chris was so wounded in his childhood that he never could deal with emotional pain very well. Over the years, Chris demonstrated again and again his need to escape from going through emotional pain. I watched him run away from hurt and loss enough times to know that the pain of our parting was likely to be more than he could face.

Chris answered the phone right away. It was so good to hear his voice once again and to hear him say my name. Molly. That was his pet name for me.

"I want to come see you and Santana."

So that's why he was calling.

Santana was our canine child. Chris called him his "boy". We both very much loved the little Chihuahua that Chris had brought home to me 8 years before. When we separated, I told Chris that he could have any or all of our possessions. But Santana, I could not live without. Chris didn't know where he was headed or even where he would live. How could he care for our precious little dog? Still, I wondered whether Chris would give me any trouble about giving me full custody of his "boy". He never did. On the day that we went our separate ways, the last thing he said to me in person was,

"Take care of my boy."

As I thought about Chris' request to come to see us, I was so conflicted. My heart ached to see him—to be with this man whom I had walked through life with for more than thirty years. How I missed him. Still, for me, the wounds of our separation were still so painfully raw. I wasn't sure if I could see Chris and not give in to our living together again. I felt it unwise for us to get back together, at least right now.

For weeks after Chris' departure, Santana lay on the back of our leather sofa, looking out the living room window watching and waiting for Chris to come home. Of course, he never did. During those weeks, not only did I feel my own heart breaking, but I had to watch Santana's heart breaking, too. My head and my heart fought it out. I hesitantly gave Chris my answer.

"Chris, it was so hard on both of us after you left. I'm not sure it would be wise for us to see each other yet for my sake and for Santana's sake, too. Maybe we should wait a little longer. A few more months or so and then see how we feel?"

I was relieved when Chris went along.

"Okay, just think about it and let me know when I can come. You have my new cell number now, so just call me when you decide. Tell Nellie I said hi. Have a wonderful time together."

It was an upbeat conversation. I felt so positive about "us". We said goodbye and I hung up the phone.

In 2005, Chris and I had moved to Pennsylvania after living in Atlanta, Georgia, for twenty-seven years. I had been the one to initiate the move for business reasons. We both considered our new location a temporary one. It was part of our larger life plan to move to Durango, Colorado.

Chris and I had chosen Durango together as our place. We had visited Durango in 2004 on our 25th wedding anniversary trip. As we walked down Durango's

Main Avenue, almost immediately and in unison, we looked at each other and said,

"This is the place."

Our mutual dream of moving west and opening a gallery to showcase Chris' southwestern, Native American art was close to coming true. We bought a small piece of property just outside of Durango, north of town. At that time in our lives, it felt as if things couldn't have been much better.

It was the voice of Officer Gallegos that dragged me away from my memories and back into the present. Now the officer wanted to know why I thought Chris might have considered suicide. And he wanted clarification on our relationship—my living in Durango and Chris in Taos. This continued interrogation was forcing me to think about answers to his questions and the thinking brought back all the pain of my current reality.

I explained that Chris and I were separated after being together for thirty years; Chris had a history of depression; Chris had attempted suicide many years ago; our marriage had fallen apart just three and a half months before. After the separation, Chris had relocated to Taos. I had moved to Durango.

"But I just talked to him six days ago, officer."

My body was beginning to react now to all the questions, the answers, and the possibility that Chris had hurt himself. My stomach and my chest tightened.

The officer explained that since Chris' truck was left at the gorge bridge, a place known for suicides, containing his clothing, art work, fishing gear, a wallet, cell phone, a pair of glasses and a pack of cigarettes, it was clear that they would have to look into where Chris might be or what might have happened to him. One of the Native vendors who sells crafts at the gorge reported that the truck had been parked there for two days but no one had been seen around it.

"Your husband is nowhere to be found."

While we talked, I tried to visualize the Rio Grande Gorge Bridge, the truck, and the details as the officer explained them. Chris and I had driven across that bridge on our trip to Durango several years before. The gorge was breathtakingly beautiful and deep. Back then, as we approached it by car, the wide-open desert and highway curves disappeared behind us and without warning we were on top of the bridge surrounded by the immense gorge below.

Chris and I had pulled into the parking lot nearby, the same parking lot where the officer was describing that Chris' truck was found. On that drive together, we walked out on the bridge along a scenic walkway so we could look down into the gorge and at the river running through it some amazing 650 feet below us.

Now being told that Chris' truck had been abandoned there at this very bridge for two days and that he was nowhere to be found brought me sheer panic. It was in that instant that I knew. I had to go to Taos. I told the officer that I would be there first thing in the morning.

As I hung up the phone, a helpless, sinking feeling came over me. I sat at the desk in my home office, numb. From where I sat, I looked through the bedroom door at Santana, all curled up on the bed. I wondered what I should do now.

So I called Chris' sister, Mary Jo. I dialed her number, not thinking about what time it was in Dallas. Thankfully, Mary Jo's husband, John, immediately answered my call.

"John, this is Mary. I just got a call from the New Mexico State Police saying that Chris is missing."

There was no surprise. The police had called them, too, tracking them down through their daughter Aimee from her number saved in Chris' cell phone. I was concerned about Aimee having to take that call and how frightening that must have been for her.

"I am going to Taos early in the morning, John. I will keep you posted on what I find."

I crawled back into bed with Santana. There was nothing I could do until morning. I was overwhelmed with thoughts of what the next day might bring. As I tossed and turned, waiting impatiently for the break of dawn, I somehow fell asleep and into a dream.

I saw Chris on the second floor of a building. It was not a building that I recognized. Chris was crouched down in a space under the floor, accessible by a drop door. There were several women in the room above the space. One of the women had a broom in her hand, sweeping. I was confused as to whether Chris had chosen to hide in that space for a couple of days or whether the women were hiding him there. Were they protecting him? I woke up, wondering.

I lay there thinking about what the dream could mean. I wanted to believe the dream meant that Chris was somewhere safe, just hiding out and would show up again in a couple of days. I drew Santana closer to me and we cuddled listening to the night sounds making their way through my open bedroom window. Past memories of Chris taking off for days at a time, literally disappearing when he felt depressed, played back in my head. Maybe this was just a repeat of one of those times. The energy it took to waiver back and forth between hope and despair was just too much. There would be no more sleep tonight. I decided to get up and start my long drive to Taos.

I took Santana out for a quick walk around the block, showered and dressed, gathered up a pair of jeans and a top, threw some toiletries in a bag, got Santana's blanket and pillow and hopped into my car, holding Santana on my lap.

Most Durango mornings are crisp and beautiful and that Thursday morning was no different. The air was clean, dry and fragrant. Yet my reason for being up so early was very, very different. Santana loved to ride in the car. He was happy and cuddled up under his blanket, content to make my lap his special place for the duration of the trip.

On my way out of town, I stopped by the assisted living home where I worked to let the staff know that I was headed for Taos and the reason why. Keri, my wonderful co-worker, hugged me and encouraged me to take as much time as I needed. She agreed to cover for me until I returned. I promised to call when I knew more about just how long I might be away. It was just a little before 7 a.m.

The drive from Durango to Taos takes about four hours. I knew today it would feel much longer. Questions swirled inside me with hurricane force.

"Chris, did you do this? Why? Didn't you feel you could reach out to me? Were you in that much pain? Was your call six days ago your attempt to reach out? It didn't sound like that type of phone call. This can't be true, Chris. Please, Chris, be alive!"

I received solace only by stroking the precious canine bundle on my lap and prayed that the outcome would not be as the police suspected. I just kept saying, over and over,

"Please, Chris, be alive!"

In an attempt to calm myself and get my mind on something else for the long drive ahead, I called my sister, Nancy, who lived in Lancaster, Pennsylvania. Chris and I were particularly close to Nancy and her husband, Carl. I knew that Nancy would be able to lift my spirits somehow.

Nancy answered. I was grateful. I told her what had happened. She was as surprised and shocked as I had been, especially that the state police were involved. Nancy was concerned for me driving alone to Taos. I reassured her that I was fine and would call her the minute I saw and talked with Chris.

Initially, I felt somewhat better after getting off the phone with Nancy. Still, it didn't take long for the numbness and panic to return. I drove as fast as I safely could through southern Colorado and into northern New Mexico. On another day, I might have noticed the rolling hills dotted with yellowing aspens and the vast ranchland, plentiful with grazing cattle and horses. Today I didn't notice. Desperation to get to Chris, find him, and hear his voice again placed a tight grasp on my attention.

Once the road mile markers told me I was nearing Taos, I called the state police and let them know I was nearby. An Officer Phillip Chandler took my call. The gorge seemed the logical place to meet. The gorge was on my way into Taos. And it was where the search and rescue operation for Chris had begun. When I pulled into the gorge rest area, it was 10:45 a.m. As I parked at the end of the picnic area parking lot at the gorge, everything in me wanted to make a U-turn and simply drive away. I stayed.

As I arrived at the gorge, a uniformed officer approached my car. I introduced myself and discovered that he was Officer Phillip Chandler. A helicopter moving slowing under the bridge and through the gorge caught my attention. Officer Chandler confirmed that this was part of the search and rescue in an attempt to find Chris. The helicopter had been brought in from Santa Fe that morning. They had been searching the gorge for approximately one hour.

We stood in silence for some time, immersed in our own separate thoughts about what was happening. Our eyes followed as the helicopter moved up and down both sides of the gorge. Each time the helicopter hovered over one particular spot, I felt as if my heart would stop. Did they find something? The discomfort and anxiety took on a life of its own and forced me away from the scene and back to my car. Santana was happy to see me and grateful for a much needed walk. From the edge of the parking lot, I was able to peer over a fence and take in the magnitude of the gorge river below. I felt a heaviness and overwhelming sadness take hold. Still, I hung on to the unanswered questions that remained—and hope. I hung on to hope.

The helicopter ascended from the gorge, swirling up past us, scaring Santana. I quickly scooped him up, clutching him to my chest. The power of it unnerved us both. As I approached my car, Officer Chandler showed up with a progress report. They had now searched under the bridge, above the water and about four miles south of the bridge. Nothing was found. They would make a few more passes above and through the gorge and then terminate the search.

At first, I felt encouraged that they hadn't found anything. But then my fear and disappointment set in. How could they just abandon the effort? It didn't seem right. A few more passes and then quit? I was relieved and frustrated all at the same time. I remained silent as I processed my concerns. Just fifteen minutes later, the search and rescue effort for Chris was called off.

At that point, Officer Chandler asked me to follow him into town to the police station. I needed to file an official missing persons report. Once at the station, we completed the paperwork necessary to file the report. Then, Officer Chandler handed me an envelope. I couldn't breathe and the room caved in on me— Chris' wallet, glasses and cell phone. Officer Chandler must have noticed my reaction because the next thing I knew he was handing me a glass of water. He placed his hand on my shoulder and even though I said nothing, I felt a deep appreciation for his gesture of concern.

So there I sat in a police station in Taos, New Mexico, holding Chris' wallet, his glasses, his cell phone. But where was Chris? I rationalized fast and furious. They said his cigarettes were left behind in the truck, too. They didn't bring me his cigarettes. Chris never went anywhere without his cigarettes. So I began to fear foul play. Someone must have forced him to go. It took a while, but my thoughts calmed down and I regained my composure a bit.

According to Officer Chandler, most people who have actually jumped from the gorge bridge fall onto the dry land of the steep gorge and never hit the water. But when they do, their bodies tend to get hung up underwater, sometimes for days and later emerge and are found. I didn't want to be hearing any of this. But I felt hopeful that the officer seemed to be implying that the police might resume their search again if Chris didn't make an appearance within the next day or so.

Once my business was completed there, the gravity of the situation kept me sitting in the police department parking lot, trying to comprehend. I slowly opened the black tri-fold wallet that I had given to Chris as a Christmas gift several years earlier. I was hoping to find a note or some bit of information that might offer a clue to where I could find him. The first thing facing me was his Pennsylvania driver's license. Seeing his face, the picture on the license, made me feel weak. I slapped the wallet shut, thinking I couldn't look at his picture without going crazy. I reconsidered. I needed to do this. Briefly, setting my emotions aside, I opened the wallet again. A business card from a gallery where he reportedly worked. Twenty-seven dollars in cash. Twenty-seven dollars. We were married for exactly twenty-seven years.

Was this coincidence or a message? Fear rippled through my heart. Surely he wouldn't do anything to harm himself and then leave this as a sign for me. This was not a possibility I was ready to consider.

I closed the wallet and placed it back into the envelope with the other items, just as the officer had presented it to me. I found a quaint place to stay just down the highway from the police station called the Sagebrush Inn. They would accept pets. I got Santana settled in the room and left him there to sleep. I headed off to the gallery where Chris had his art on display and where he was reportedly working.

The gallery was called the Enchanted Dreams Foundation. It was located on Paseo del Pueblo Norte, the main street through Taos. The gallery was located just north of town. Officer Chandler had given me directions. The gallery was one of several shops in a beige-colored, two-story building. I found a parking space right in front. A small flower garden between the gallery and the sidewalk led me to the gallery entrance. The book store to the left of the gallery caught my eye. A turquoise wrought iron staircase, also to the left of the gallery, led to what appeared to be apartments on the second floor.

Once inside, I was surprised at how large the gallery space was, even though it was long and narrow. The wood floor made a strange, loud creaking sound as I stepped forward. Glass cases lined the middle of the gallery, holding Native American jewelry and some vintage/antique pieces. I hesitated after taking just a few steps inside, feeling scared and apprehensive. Those all too familiar knots started to form in my stomach. I wondered how these folks who I assumed had come to know and love Chris for the past three months would receive me. What did they know about me, the estranged wife? And what did they know about Chris' so-called disappearance?

It was natural for my eyes to be drawn immediately to Chris' artwork in the front section of the gallery. Seeing and feeling the spirit of his artwork again, I was momentarily stunned by the impact. I felt as though Chris was right there in the room with me.

I tried to re-focus on the purpose of my visit as I noticed a tall, attractive woman with shoulder-length blonde hair approaching me. I guessed that she was in her late forties. I introduced myself as Mary Cardin, Chris' wife. She was obviously shaken by hearing who I was. She reached out and hugged me. I could feel right away that she was the type of person Chris would be drawn to— attractive, strong and genuine. She introduced herself to me as Lois Fernandez, owner of the gallery. Her warm reception, her obvious shock and concern about Chris' disappearance, and her kind nature somewhat calmed my initial fear and uncertainty.

As we stood in relaxed conversation, Lois told me what she knew about Chris' disappearance up to now.

"The state police came to see me Tuesday night. They had found one of my business cards in Chris' wallet. They told me Chris was missing. I told them the last time I had seen him was Monday night. A few of us had eaten dinner together here at the gallery. It was Labor Day. Chris had painted at his easel outside the gallery for most of the day just as he had every day for the three months he'd been living here. Many people got to know him this way, because of his constant presence painting outside the gallery. They liked watching his genius at work. They marveled at how the weathered Native American faces emerged from a blank canvas."

As Lois talked, it came back to me, too, how much I loved to watch Chris create his beautiful pieces. His specialty was painting Native American faces. He always started with an oval of brown oil paint on the canvas. That oval would soon transform into the face of whatever character Chris was imagining.

Lois went on to describe the last time she saw
Chris. She had suggested that they pick up some chicken
and have a Labor Day get-together on the back porch of the
gallery. So Chris joined several other gallery artists to help
pick up the food. They all hung out on the back porch,
talked, ate, and danced to some old Beach Boys tunes. At
some point during the evening, probably between 6:30 and
7:30, Lois said she noticed Chris wasn't around anymore.
Someone had seen him just wander out as he tended to do
on many occasions. Sadness caught in Lois' voice.

"That was the last time I saw him."

I could see the distress and worry in her eyes.
Somehow trying to put her mind at ease along with my
own, I updated her on what had transpired up to now, my
experience at the gorge, the missing persons report and the
suspended search, since there was no concrete proof that
Chris did in fact jump from the bridge. I felt the need to ask
her point blank.

"Lois, do *you* think Chris committed suicide by
jumping from that bridge?"

Her answer was reassuring in some ways.

"Well, he didn't give any of us reason to think that he was that unhappy or that he was troubled in any way. So I don't know. To be honest, Chris always seemed very happy-go-lucky. He seemed to be adjusting well here. Chris had his art hanging in this main street gallery and I'd sold some of his work. Collectors were beginning to notice him. It normally takes artists many years to get to that point in this town."

I was not surprised by the report Lois gave of Chris' immediate success here in Taos due to the level of his talent. Chris was a magnificent artist. I had always known that his work would do very well if he just had the right exposure at the right location. Her response gave me hope again that Chris was still okay. That hope started a whirlwind of other viable possibilities going around in my head about where Chris might be.

Maybe he just met someone at the gorge and left his truck there for a few days. Chris loved the outdoors. Maybe he parked his truck there and took off walking across the mesa to scope out a good spot to camp and fish. Maybe he fell and hurt himself and couldn't walk back on his own. These were options that could allow me to hang on to hope for just a little longer.

Before I left the gallery, Lois shared with me that she and most of Chris' friends had assumed that he was divorced. They had no idea that he was so recently separated. Chris had apparently not shared very much of himself or his personal life with anyone in Taos except with a man named Robert. Lois explained that Robert was also an artist and had some of his work hanging in her gallery, too. Chris and Robert were both talented handy-men and loved doing work for Lois around the gallery and at her personal residence. According to Lois, Robert and Chris became instant friends, possibly because each was single and each had recently moved to Taos.

Once back at the Inn, I checked on my Santana and called Mary Jo with an update. At this point I was despondent and at a loss as to what to do next. Mary Jo's response was immediate.

"I am coming to Taos to help you look for him."

—————————————

Mary Jo planned to fly into the Albuquerque, New Mexico, airport and I would drive down to meet her. I had never made the trek from Taos to Albuquerque before. It was late and dark and so I focused on the road signs. I thought about what I might say to Chris' sister when I saw her.

Mary Jo was standing at the curb of the passenger pick-up area waiting for me. Chris' sister is almost six feet tall, very slender with short, stunning dark reddish hair. She is a person whose beauty and stately stature command attention. Mary Jo was impeccably dressed as usual. Today she wore a stylish black blouse, designer jeans and eye-catching silver jewelry.

We hugged each other in a long, tight embrace. My loneliness began to lift now, having Mary Jo here with me. As we released each other, she commented on how thin I had become. I explained what a difficult few months it had been since the separation. I told her how much I still loved Chris.

"I'm so sorry that all this is happening, Mary Jo!"

I was sorry for us both. Mary Jo reached out and pulled me to her again. There we stood, beside my car amidst the chaos of arrivals and departures, crying. Neither of us was ready to face the task ahead of us. Nonetheless, together, we headed for Taos.

Mary Jo was quiet as I drove. Along the way I slowly eked out the day's events at the gorge and at the gallery. I shared what information I had and held back the "what ifs". Mary Jo had visited Chris just two weeks before in Taos. She did say that Chris had not given her any indication that anything was bothering him.

Mary Jo knew some of the details of my separation from Chris. He had spent a few days with her in Dallas after we separated on his trip west. Mary Jo was the only friend or family member Chris had made contact with after our separation. Once she heard from Chris, Mary Jo had let me know that Chris was okay and that he was planning to head to New Mexico to find a new place to live. I was grateful for this. I told Mary Jo that I didn't need to know who he was with, exactly where he was, or what he was doing. I just needed to know that he was okay.

Now as we drove to Taos, I felt at some point, I would owe Mary Jo more details of our separation. I knew I would share the whole story. But at this moment, all I wanted her to know was that even though I had asked Chris to leave, I still loved him very much, that my constant prayer for him after we separated was that God would put the right people in his path, that he would be safe and that he would be healed from all his internal wounds.

As the trip wore on, a comfortable silence settled in for both of us. We'd have plenty of time to talk more when we arrived in Taos. I welcomed the quiet time, alone again with my memories.

As I drove along in silence, I found myself reflecting back over the years when Chris and I were together; over our childhoods and our upbringings that had such a profound influence on why our two wounded spirits were so attracted to each other. Through the maze of thought, what lingered were the painful precipitating events that prompted me to ask Chris to leave just three and a half months before.

Mary L. Cardin

Chapter Two

Betrayal

"I think I'll take the Harley and go to Atlanta for the weekend. I've been wanting to go back and ride up to Helen again. I miss it there."

Helen is a quaint little town north of Atlanta where we used to ride the Harley on weekends. We both loved it in Helen and I understood why he could be missing it.

It was May 2007 when Chris approached me about taking the trip.

I had wanted to be supportive, so I told Chris he should go and have a good time. Still, I felt somewhat suspicious about these particular trip plans. Chris had had an extramarital affair early in our marriage. And then there were several indiscretions over time throughout our marriage, always as a result of Chris' ongoing bouts of depression. After a long time and a great deal of pain, it felt as though we had resolved the issues and were able to move on in our marriage.

Over the course of our thirty-year relationship, Chris continued to battle ongoing cyclical episodes of depression, usually preceded by what was referred to as a manic stage. Chris would always tell me that he could handle the depression on his own, never seeking counseling or treatment. I had chosen to believe him because normally, he did in fact, handle these challenging times effectively on his own. Chris would eventually work through his symptoms and return to being my loving and creative husband. Chris often remained depression-free for several years at a time. But while immersed in these depressive states, indiscretion was too often Chris' reaction.

I loved Chris. Intellectually, I understood why he did the things he did. That is why I had been willing to stay with him—and wait for him until he returned to the wonderful, loving and talented man that I had fallen in love with. I thought that if I loved him enough, I could fix him.

I thought my love for him would be enough. I just wanted to love Chris enough to make him feel that he finally belonged—that someone *did* truly love him—someone who would stay with him and not abandon him, no matter what. It hurt me badly when he acted that way. I knew that what Chris did was unacceptable behavior, but I loved him. I understood.

So when Chris announced his plans to ride his Harley to Atlanta, I knew something was up. How I hated re-experiencing those old familiar and painful emotions of fear and suspicion. Sure, we both missed beautiful Helen, Georgia, and we missed Atlanta and our friends there. Neither of us was enjoying the weather in Pittsburgh. It was only after our move that we learned that Pittsburgh's weather rivals that of Seattle, Washington, in a competition for the least amount of sunshine it has to offer.

In Atlanta, our house had frequently been the center of socializing for our close community of neighbors. There were always folks visiting us. There was a party going on somewhere in the neighborhood most every weekend. When we moved from Atlanta to the Pittsburgh area, we rented a little two-bedroom house on two acres. The house backed up to a golf course, with no neighbors in sight. So Chris and I had gone from having a very active social life to being almost totally isolated. In hindsight, neither of us had given any thought to the impact that the combination of seclusion and gloomy weather would have on us individually and on our relationship.

Even though I felt so uncomfortable with Chris returning to Atlanta and to our old neighborhood without me, we were never the kind to tell each other what we could or couldn't do. That was one of the many things that I loved about Chris and our relationship. So off he went to Atlanta on his Harley.

Chris called me to let me know he had arrived in Atlanta safely. He was hanging out with some of our old neighbors. They hosted a cookout in his honor. He said everyone had asked about me. He said he was having a great time. I was pleased and happy for him. But for the three days he was away, that nagging *I just know something's going to happen* feeling permeated my every thought.

I certainly knew enough about the power of thought to question myself as to whether I *wanted* something to happen. I realized that in thinking so much about my fear of betrayal, I was giving a huge amount of power to it.

Chris arrived home late, so his first night home, we hadn't talked much about his trip. However, the next evening as we sat down for dinner, I looked across the table and into Chris' eyes and began the conversation that ended our marriage.

"Is there anything you want to tell me about your trip to Georgia?"

Initially, Chris seemed surprised by my question, but then soon realized that I instinctively knew something wasn't right. He confirmed my suspicions.

"Yes, I slept with Sophie one of the nights I was there."

Even though my heart had already known the truth, the reality of it was still so painful. Chris' confession had just transformed my fear into reality. Sophie was someone we had both known as a friend for many years.

For a moment I wondered what I should do. But I knew what had to come next.

"But I thought I had made it perfectly clear to you that if this ever happened again, it was over between us. Didn't I, Chris?"

The pain and anguish in his face in that brief moment mirrored back the pain and anguish in my own heart. Maybe it would have been better if he hadn't been so honest. Had I really wanted him to tell me the truth?

The dining room where we sat together suddenly became small. An eerie silence filled the tightening space. My emotions were all over the board. Could I, or even should I, forgive him just one more time? Maybe I should continue to try and make this marriage work? Did I really want our thirty-year relationship to end over a one night stand?

Still, in spite of all the questions and justification, I knew deep down inside that I had to be true to myself. I had grown into a healthy woman and had begun to live by a set of spiritual principles. I had resolved to stop being a victim in my life and to live within a healthy relationship. It didn't really feel like a choice. I was no longer a woman who could accept betrayal as a part of my relationship with Chris.

I could barely speak the words that my heart forced up into my throat.

"Chris, I'm done! I'm really done this time."

I looked down at my left hand and examined the silver wedding ring that I had worn for so many years. I sadly and slowly removed it. I tried to hand it to Chris but he wouldn't take it. I gently reached over to where Chris was sitting and placed the ring on his knee. That simple act and the meaning behind it stunned us both.

As my throat tightened and burned, the tears streamed down my face. I mumbled,

"I hope it was worth it!"

"No! No, it wasn't!"

That was all that he could get out as he sat there, still clearly not quite believing what I had just done. Neither of us believed any of this at that moment. Our marriage was over. Without giving it any thought, I managed to tell Chris that I was going to drive over to Lancaster to my sister's on Friday and stay for the weekend. I asked him if he would be able to be gone by the time I got back from my sister's.

I knew that I would not be able to watch as he packed his things. And I definitely could not watch Christopher Lyle Cardin, the love of my life, just drive away.

It took a while. Finally he answered.

"Yes, I can do that. I don't know where I'll go, but I can be gone by Sunday."

With that, I got up, still crying, my body shaking, and took my dinner plate to the kitchen. Dusk was just settling in and the final moments of sunlight were streaming through the bay window in the kitchen casting a peaceful, shadowy hue over the kitchen. Following my lead, Chris cleared his plate, too and the place where he always sat already looked too empty. He came close to me in the kitchen standing by the sink. He wrapped his strong arms around me and held me. Neither of us said a word, as together we felt the pain of two hearts tearing apart.

As we lay in bed that night, I cried. Chris held and comforted me throughout the night. The man I had just asked to get out of my life, with no anger and no pleading, comforted me. This didn't seem right. This was not the way it should be. Somewhere in the night, we made love. Bittersweet love.

The next day would be our last day together. Not knowing how I would make it through, I got up and went to work. When I arrived home later that evening, Chris was in the garage, sorting through some of his tools and fishing gear. Seeing Chris take steps toward leaving sent a ripple of doubt through my mind. Had I made the right decision? It all felt so final now. However, both of us managed to gather our emotions, and we had dinner together again that evening. Chris talked about the things he planned to take with him, things that he planned to leave behind, things that he didn't want anymore. He did some thinking out loud about where he might go. At that point, he still didn't have any definite plans.

"All I know is that I'm taking what I can in the truck—all my art and some personal belongings. That's all. You can have everything else."

"Chris, you know I don't care about material things. You can have anything you want in the house. Just take it."

"No," was his adamant response. "I don't care about things either. I'm just taking what I can fit in the truck. Do with the rest as you wish."

I had always loved Chris' art. The realization that he was planning to take all of his artwork with him sent a jolt of regret through me. I loved being surrounded by his passion, his talent, and his genius. This beautiful energy had filled our home one piece at a time over the years. His love for his Native American ancestors came alive in his paintings and that love had surrounded me, too. Being part Cherokee, Chris' paternal grandmother had instilled the love of the People in him at a very early age.

Chris possessed a God-given gift. This talent was not something he had learned from any one person or at any school. He was born with it. Now, the thought of not seeing Chris standing at his easel, pouring his soul onto the canvas made me feel as though he was taking a part of my soul with him, embedded in that canvas. I knew I was giving up so much, and yet I also knew that I had to trust what my heart was telling me I had to do. So, for the last time, we went to bed together that night. And in the midst of his tears and mine, both dreading the morning, we made love once again, for the very last time.

Our love making was intense that night, hard, rough and demanding. It was as if we both knew it was the last time we would love together that way and there was almost a desperation to it. Still, it was beautiful.

The morning found me wanting to stay in Chris' arms, against his warm body in the bed we had shared for so many years. Instead, with my personal items for the weekend in hand, and Santana on his leash, I walked out the front door though the little screened-in porch and out to my car. Standing in the driveway, I noticed that it was a fairly sunny day for May in Pennsylvania. I wondered where Chris was and how I could possibly say goodbye.

I found Chris at his truck, the black Chevy Avalanche, loading his Harley.

"Are you taking that with you?"

"No," he told me. "Dave bought it and I'm taking it over to him."

Chris had sold his prize possession. His custom built Harley. Chris had invested so much time, money and quite a lot of himself into building that bike. My heart broke for him. How could I do this to him? I could feel my resolve weakening. But then my mind quickly jerked back to reality, and to the reason why I had asked him to leave. I knew I had to stick to my decision.

My mind embraced the thought that this may be the last time I would ever see Chris. His 6' 2" frame looked so good in his jeans and black Harley T-shirt. His face was void of emotion. This was the familiar face of Chris, whenever he tried to cover his pain. I stood next to him, reached up, stroked the back of his shaven head and put my arms around his neck. We hugged, and then briefly kissed our final kiss. I had always loved the feel of him, his tall, dark lean body, his strong arms around me, his lips against mine. The kiss was gentle and brief—a little distant and detached for both of us. I knew that I would miss him terribly. I did not know then that this would be the last time I would ever touch him.

Chris reached down and picked up Santana. He held our little canine for a moment, kissed him and said to me,

"Take good care of my boy."

I walked away from him slowly, across the yard toward my car. I was sobbing uncontrollably and wondered how I would make the drive to my sister's house in this state of mind. As I backed my car out of the driveway, Chris and I just looked at each other. With the most devastating, lost feeling that I had ever experienced, I slowly put my hand in the air, sending out a half-hearted wave. Then, I pulled out onto the road and drove away.

The four-hour drive to and from Lancaster was pretty much a blur. I held Santana tight. Our little dog had no idea what was happening in our lives.

It was heart wrenching to tell my sister and her
family that I had just asked Chris to leave. Chris and I had
always been especially close to my sister Nancy and her
husband Carl and their two children, Julie and Jeremy. As
always, they were very supportive, they understood my
decision, and compassionately expressed their concern for
Chris, too.

I didn't know what to expect when I retuned from
Lancaster two days later. It was Sunday evening as I
arrived at the house that had been our home. I wondered
whether he was really gone. As I drove into the upper
driveway to the front of our little two-story brick house,
everything was dark. No lights were on inside. Chris' truck
was gone. There was a part of me that wanted him to still
be there, waiting for me.

As I walked through the screened-in porch and into
the house I was hit hard by the dark and quiet that was
waiting for me there. I was alone. I reached around the
corner, feeling for the light switch. The living room light
came on, showing me that there was no one there. It didn't
feel like home here anymore. As I turned on the kitchen

light, I noticed something lying on the kitchen counter by the backdoor. My eyes focused on what Chris had left behind—our wedding rings. No note. Nothing. Just our wedding rings. I lay my head down on the counter, next to the rings and sobbed. What had I done?

So why was that the pivotal moment when every part of me knew it was time to say no more and reclaim my human dignity in my relationship with Chris?

Before then, I had allowed my own past experiences and Chris' to drive our present and our future together. Chris' mother had suffered and battled with the same shift between periods of mania and depression that Chris so often displayed. Both Chris and his mother were enormously creative and intelligent human beings who were blessed with huge talents, yet pained with this dark side. I had a deep understanding and empathy for their struggle.

Chris' birth parents had divorced when Chris was around three years old. Chris and his older brother went to live with their father. Chris' sister, Mary Jo went to live with their mother. Chris expressed to me many times over our years together the pain and trauma he experienced, calling out for his mother—being told that his mother didn't love him. He never let go of the thought that his mother had abandoned him.

As adults, Chris and his mother mended their relationship to some extent but his deep yearning for love never let go of him. This contributed to Chris' acting out in his future relationships with women. We often talked about the fact that his womanizing was most likely a symptom of his subconsciously looking for his mother's love.

Then, when Chris was seventeen, his father and step-mother were killed in a private airplane crash. Through Chris' eyes, at that moment, he was a child again and his father had abandoned him, too. This tragic incident reawakened the abandonment issues that he had been struggling with in his early childhood years. His wounding continued and the seeds of depression were planted, establishing deep, strong roots within him. From that time on, Chris admittedly rebelled against everything that society considered the norm—including God and religion and healthy, committed relationships.

My own religious upbringing and both childhood and adult trauma also impacted the way I dealt with issues in my marriage for a long time. I was the youngest of ten children born into a Mennonite family, a conservative Christian faith, akin to the Amish religion. My father was the Deacon of the church that we attended. Consequently, we were raised in a fairly strict religious environment. We were told not to question what we were taught.

I so respected and loved my father and I mean no disrespect now when I say that I wasn't taught the loving, joyful and powerful side of God as a child, or at least I don't remember it if I was. What I do remember is the fear-based side of the teachings. We were told to do or not do things, but we were never given the spiritual reasons as to why we should or should not do them.

I don't fault my father for this. Possibly this was his experience growing up. These belief systems tend to be passed on generation after generation. Nevertheless, growing up, I received the message that you make your marriage work at all costs. Since, in my family, so much emphasis was placed on appearances, divorce simply was not an option. As a result, I kept the ongoing issues in my marriage a secret from my family.

Betrayal seemed to be an ongoing issue for me from childhood to adulthood, not just in my relationship with Chris. My innocence was taken from me early in my childhood. I was around 6 or 7 years old. I knew I couldn't tell my parents. That was the first painful secret that my upbringing had forced me to hold inside. I held that secret alone for the majority of my life.

As an adult, I experienced several business betrayals, too. Later I discovered that I had learned to play the victim role in all these situations. The victim role spilled over into many other areas of my life, including my relationship with Chris. One of the gifts that I received as a result of one betrayal in the business world was an open door to a new career and my true calling. This happened just six months prior to my separation from Chris. In the midst of my frustration and to take my mind off my own painful business situation, I decided to take a position with a local in-home senior care agency. I just needed to be of service. I asked to be assigned to someone who needed assistance—someone I could care for. I was assigned to a wonderful woman named Georgianne.

Within the first several days of being with Georgianne, I knew without a doubt that I was now doing the work that I was supposed to do versus working in the corporate world as I had in the past. Consequently, my new, inspired career—caring for the elderly was born. I now had purpose in my life—serving others instead of focusing on myself. This transition also provided a stepping stone to my rightful spiritual path—and my decision to never be a victim in my life ever again.

———————

After Chris' departure, I took a month or so to process and grieve the ending of our marriage. Along with the introspection time, I busied myself sorting through all of our belongings. After more than thirty years together, we had accumulated a great deal of "stuff" and now I found myself having to sadly un-separate us and our belongings.

I also allowed this time to unfold naturally, so that I could determine where Chris would eventually land. I knew we both loved Durango, Colorado. I certainly didn't want to move to Durango if Chris felt he needed to make Durango his new home. So patiently, I stayed behind with Santana, in the little two-story brick house on the golf course in Pennsylvania until I learned that Chris had chosen his location. Two weeks passed before I learned from Chris' sister Mary Jo that he had chosen Taos, New Mexico, as his new location. Chris' choice had made my decision clear for me. Durango would be my new home. I moved there in July of 2007, just two months after our separation.

Once again, my sister, Nancy was there for me. She joined me and Santana for the three-day trip from Pennsylvania to Durango. I had arranged for my possessions to be shipped and they were delivered just one day after Nancy and I arrived at my new rental house. I had found a charming two-story 1881 Victorian house on the corner of 10th Street and the Historic E. 3rd Avenue. My new surroundings were exactly as I had envisioned them— a dream come true in many ways. The house was situated on a well maintained tree-lined street with lovely homes and friendly people. It was just two blocks from my front door to Durango's historic Main Avenue. This charming and active small town is considered one of America's top twelve distinguished destinations.

I had purposely decided to live in town rather than choosing a more rural location. I only knew one person in Durango at that time and didn't want to isolate myself. Since I was starting over in life, just me and my Santana, I thought it would be healthy for me to surround myself with people and activity.

As Mary Jo and I headed from the Albuquerque airport toward Taos, all that had happened in the past seemed like lifetimes ago. Time had warped somehow and everything felt so surreal. Mary Jo and I would begin our search for Chris the following day. Mary Jo remained quiet and alone with her thoughts for most of the drive. I found myself wanting to talk more about Chris. I wanted to ask her what she felt might have happened to him. But as I looked over at her so engrossed in her own world of thoughts, I decided against it. I allowed her to process all of it in her own way. Her brother was missing. She was here to help me search for him. So I drove and sat alone with my silent reflections until we arrived back at the Sagebrush Inn and tried to prepare for tomorrow.

Mary L. Cardin

Chapter Three

Beginning the Search

On Friday morning, I introduced Mary Jo to the Enchanted Dreams Foundation Gallery, and to Lois. Lois told us about several of Chris' friends in town—people who Chris had become particularly close to during his short time in Taos. There was a guy named Ben. Chris, I discovered, referred to him as Medicine Man Ben. And then there was his friend, Robert. Lois suggested we might want to talk to them. Perhaps they could offer some insight into Chris' whereabouts.

Before we left the gallery, Lois gave us Ben's phone number. Mary Jo immediately called him and we arranged to meet at the Taos Inn across the street from the gallery. This was a place where Ben said that he and Chris liked to go to listen to music and have a drink. Chris always loved outdoor patio settings. I could easily picture him hanging out there at this little spirit filled Inn.

Ben was a tall, slim man with long black hair and dark skin. He did, in fact, appear to resemble how I thought a Medicine Man might look. He was anxious to speak with us, too, and we spent much of the afternoon together. However, after several hours of conversation, Ben couldn't really shed any light on where Chris might be or what he might have done. After thanking Ben for his time, Mary Jo and I went back to the state police station to make yet another attempt at convincing them to resume their search for Chris. Their decision to stop searching had been an ongoing struggle for me.

Mary Jo and I sat in the small, sparsely-furnished waiting room for almost 30 minutes before anyone at the police station could talk with us. When we finally met with an officer, we were again told that nothing more was being done or could be done unless additional evidence turned

up. I was dumbfounded to hear this. How could new
evidence turn up if nothing was being done to find it? But
by that time, I was too numb to become outwardly upset or
to even react.

Apparently, there have been many deaths by
suicide at the gorge bridge over the years. Still, there were
just as many cases of people making it look as though they
had committed suicide by jumping off the bridge but
instead were found much later in another state under a
new identity. Those incidents tended to discourage the
state police from spending too much time or resources in
search for any one person.

I was frustrated by the information but also by the
lack of resources that I had to initiate a search for Chris on
my own. The state police had the resources, but were
refusing to provide them. I tried to convince the officer
that, as far as I knew, Chris would have no reason to want
to change his identity. His identity was his life and his art.
But in the end, I was unsuccessful in my efforts and the
search and rescue for Chris remained suspended
indefinitely. It would be up to me and Mary Jo to conduct

our own search and rescue if any searching or rescuing was to be done.

By the time we left the police station, it was late in the day. The sun was starting to set over this desert town— a place that possessed an unspeakable beauty. Yet on this September day, there was a palpable flow of negative energy in the air that I found unsettling.

Mary Jo and I cleared our minds with a walk with Santana and a meal together at the Sagebrush Inn. Over dinner, we discussed many options and strategies. The idea that made most sense to both of us was to get a good night's rest, if at all possible, and then to conduct a search on foot of both rims of the gorge first thing in the morning. We called Ben and asked if he might be able to join us in the search. He agreed. We would meet at the gallery at 10 a.m.

When we arrived to meet Ben, I was surprised but pleased to learn from Lois that Chris' other close friend and fellow artist, Robert, was also planning to join us in the search. Since I had yet to meet Robert, I didn't quite know what to expect. I wondered about the kind of person he might be. I wondered whether he had been a good friend to Chris. The moment we met, my questions and concerns melted away. Robert's gentle eyes told me of his sincerity and of his level of concern about Chris and his whereabouts.

Robert had that typical "artist" look about him— that carefree attitude. Robert had dark shoulder length hair with a touch of gray running through it. He was tall, about 6 feet, and in good physical shape. Robert, like Chris, had a mysterious demeanor about him which was very intriguing to me. I was immediately at ease with him and knew that he was someone I could trust.

When Robert and I had a moment to speak privately, I asked him when he last saw or talked to Chris. It had been Monday morning, Labor Day. Chris was in front of the gallery painting as usual when Robert and his new girlfriend drove up in her car. Chris came over to the side of the car and knelt down at the passenger window where Robert was seated. Chris rested his head on Robert's arm, then turned his head and looked up at him. Robert said he noticed what he thought was a tear in Chris' eye. Robert shared with me that he was aware of the sadness and loneliness Chris had been feeling since he had come to Taos. Chris had confided in Robert. He said that he missed me and Santana and all that he had previously known as home. Chris felt that all he had left of home was what he had packed into his truck. Robert said that he felt both sadness and anger coming from Chris as he spoke of the home he had lost.

Robert's revelation ripped through my heart. All along I had suspected how Chris might have felt, but actually hearing all this confirmed by Robert broke my heart all over again. I knew I was Chris' "home" and his rock and that he always loved me and Santana with all his heart, the best that he could.

I asked Robert if he thought at the time that Chris was sad enough to commit suicide. Robert assured me that even though he knew Chris was sad and lonely, that he didn't really see any signs of his being suicidal at the time. The tear in Chris' eye did give Robert some concern. But he had dismissed it as a momentary thing and figured he'd bring it up with Chris privately sometime later in the week. Robert said he confirmed plans with Chris for a get-together the following Friday at Robert's house. Chris said he'd be there. Robert left the gallery on Monday believing that he'd see Chris on Friday.

I hesitantly asked Robert to be candid with me. Where did he think Chris was? What did he think had happened to him? Robert answered by telling me about a dream he had had about Chris Wednesday night, before he knew that Chris' truck had been found at the gorge. In his dream, Robert saw Chris standing and facing what appeared to be a fence. Chris had both hands on the fence and was staring out over the fence and into the night. It was clear that Chris wanted to jump, but he was frightened. So to ease his own fear, Chris convinced himself that he was just jumping over a short fence. Chris then hesitated momentarily, and jumped with his arms outstretched, as if he were flying.

When Robert woke up from the dream he was shaken, but didn't dwell on it much. At the time, he didn't have any reason to believe that anything had happened to

Chris. But the next morning, when Lois told Robert that Chris' truck had been found at the bridge and that it had been there for two days, Robert instantly recalled the dream. He understood then, that the dream was a message. Robert felt that he knew what had happened to Chris. He immediately drove out to the bridge that day, Thursday. He parked in the parking lot where the vendors set up their goods, walked toward the fence and noticed a man's boot turned upside down on one of the fence posts. Knowing Chris as he did, he felt that this was symbolic as a grave marker. Robert believed that it was Chris' boot that he had discovered and that Chris had placed it there.

His grave marker?

Later I would learn that using a boot as a grave marker had become a custom during the civil war. If a soldier had to be buried where he had fallen, his boot and often helmet and rifle were used to mark the grave so his body could be found later.

At the time, I was physically and emotionally shaken by Robert's story. I wondered if there really was a dream at all or whether Robert knew something more. Suspicion moved in as a way to deny what I had heard.

Maybe Robert was involved in Chris' disappearance somehow. Did Chris confide in Robert about his plans to jump? I couldn't stop the barrage of negative thoughts for quite a long while. But soon enough I had to believe my own intuition about Robert. He seemed genuine and honest. I believed his story. But, in doing so, it became harder to hold on to hope.

Also at the gallery that morning, I met Sylvia, another friend of Lois'. Sylvia had long, beautiful dark hair, and sat quietly watching the interactions between Ben, Robert, Lois, Mary Jo and I. Finally, she got up from where she was seated at the counter and slowly walked over to me. Without any warning or introductory small talk she simply stated,

"Chris has crossed over."

My body flooded with adrenalin. Did this woman mean that Chris had died? I managed to ask her that question. She answered, seemingly certain.

"Yes."

My sobs were uncontrollable for a while before I could question her any more. Eventually, Sylvia would explain.

According to Sylvia, because of the state of the universe, there was a window of opportunity to leave this earth presented to Chris. Chris had chosen to take the opportunity. Sylvia said that Chris knew that he could do more good from the other side than he could from this side, living his life on earth. Sylvia very cautiously offered the next bit information. Slowly, and watching for my reaction, she told me what else was true for her. Chris was standing there in the room with us.

My legs felt as though they would no longer hold me up. Sylvia gently put her arms around me and supported me as we walked over to the place in the room where she said Chris was waiting. My unspoken thought as we moved across the room was that if Chris was really gone, and if this was genuine and real, the only question I had for Chris right now is whether he knew how much I loved him.

Sylvia said there was something important that Chris wanted me to know. He wanted me to continue his art legacy. And I should continue journaling so that he could speak to me through my journal. How did Sylvia know I kept a journal? The skeptic in me had questions but I was beginning to believe what this woman had to say.

Then all at once, she dispelled all my disbelief. Sylvia said that Chris was in front of me, down on one knee, sweetly looking up at me. Sylvia said he was telling me that, yes, he knew how much I loved him. He said I was his shining star.

Chris had answered the only question that weighed heavy on my heart. He had called me by a name that he had given to me to represent what I had meant to him in this life—his shining star. I could no longer hold back all the tears that I had stored up inside since the initial state police phone call on Wednesday night. Sylvia lovingly held me in her arms as I freely let the emotions flow for what seemed like a very long time.

Though some denial and questions remained, after what Robert and Sylvia had told me, I began to believe that Chris was dead. That he had indeed crossed over. Now all there was left to do was find him. We took my car. Mary Jo, Robert, Ben and I drove out to the gorge north of town. We decided to search the west rim on foot first. It was an eerie feeling for me as I returned to this spot again, especially in light of the new, horrifying images and potential truths that I carried in my head.

The sun was bright and the day was hot. We knew that we couldn't stay out all day, but we wanted to do all we could to search the area for Chris this first day. Robert brought along a pair of binoculars. We used them to scan both sides of the gorge and the areas down the river for approximately one mile.

Ben's statement was matter of fact.

"We need to look for vultures and follow them."

I felt sick and wasn't sure I could continue. We stopped for a few minutes so I could recover. The possibility of Chris' body, down in that gorge, vultures picking at him, was too much for me to bear. Still, I knew what Ben said was true. If a body was down there, there would be vultures hovering around. I said a silent prayer.

"Oh, please God, if he's down there, we must find him soon."

After several hours of a physically and emotionally grueling search, we found nothing. I turned to Robert and asked,

"Do you know of anyone that I can hire to take me down the river to search?"

I just knew that I had to go down into that gorge. I had to satisfy my need to do everything that could be done to find Chris. Robert was kind, helpful and offered some possibilities.

"I know several rafting companies in town. I'll make some calls as soon as I get home tonight."

Sure enough, later that night, after trying several companies, Robert found one rafting company, Los Rios River Runners, willing to take me down the river. But they stressed how dangerous an endeavor like this one would be. Despite the danger warnings, I called them that night to set up the rafting search for the following morning. I wanted and needed to go down into that gorge as soon as possible. The owner of the rafting company set out our itinerary.

"Meet us at the boathouse at 8:45 a.m. and we'll start out from there. We can be on the river by 10:00."

The owner continued to emphasize how dangerous river rafting was at this time of the year because the water levels were so low. The last rafting trip of the year had been the previous weekend, Labor Day weekend.

"So if we don't go down the river and look for him now, no other rafters will be going down again until spring."

I had to do this now. I had to look for Chris. I could not leave Taos without knowing where Chris was or what happened to him. If he was down there, I could not leave him there all winter long.

My heart was filled with gratitude to the Los Rios River Runners for agreeing to take me down the river, and yet I was broken as I thought of the task ahead. I didn't know if I had the strength to do this and then to face the worst if we found him. Mary Jo had her own perspective as we made the search plans for the next day.

"I don't want to believe that my brother jumped off that bridge. I'm going to stay at the hotel while you go down. Is that okay with you?"

I suspected that Mary Jo chose to stay behind because if we did find her brother down in that gorge, she didn't want that to be her last image of him.

"Sure, you stay here and watch Santana for me. I can't leave Taos without knowing where he is, Mary Jo, and what's happened to him."

We understood each other's intense feelings and emotions and respected one another's individual needs in this unfathomable situation. In the morning, we hugged and I left to the boathouse. Both Robert and Ben had expressed a desire to go down the river with me, so I reserved a spot for them, too. I was so grateful for their loving support and presence.

I still wasn't sure about my strength to follow through. My hands shook and my heart pounded hard. My body was telling me this was a really bad idea. My stomach ached from lack of food over the past several days. I didn't know if I was physically strong enough to make this trip down the river. Still, I promised all of them that I was.

When I arrived at the boathouse, the rafting staff had the company van loaded with the necessary gear and rafts. Without much discussion, I paid for the trip and made my way outside and onto the van. The staff didn't quite know what to say to me. I felt their discomfort, but I also understood. This would be no ordinary rafting trip.

Mary L. Cardin

Chapter Four

Strength to Survive

Nothing could have prepared me for that trip down the river and the strength I would need to survive the weeks and months that would follow were it not for the spiritual path I had discovered prior to my separation from Chris.

Authors and inspirational speakers such as Eckhart Tolle, Wayne Dyer, Robert Scheinfeld, Gregg Braden and Joel Osteen became the foundation of my spiritual study. I felt like a sponge and I soaked up everything. I began to put into practice what I learned.

I mentally sent loving thoughts to people who upset me, not letting it matter who was right or wrong. I trusted my spirit for guidance and clarity and began to let life unfold just the way it should. I let go of my ego so much more often. I learned to replace negative thoughts with positive ones. I felt truly connected to God.

I slowly transformed my old ways of thinking and of living. My new understanding exposed my unhealthy thought process. I recognized how much of my personal power that I had given to those who I felt had betrayed me over the years. I began to see those people as gifts in my life because they had given me the opportunity to discover an amazing inner strength that I didn't even know I had. I learned that once I reclaimed my power, those who had betrayed me would be out of my life. I was alarmed when I first heard this concept. I began to suspect that Chris might be one of the people that would ultimately have to go away, too.

As a way of turning inward and staying connected, as part of my spiritual journey, I learned to schedule quiet meditative and prayer time. I would get out of bed late at night, sit in the dark, yoga-style on the floor in the middle of our living room. This practice would quiet my mind. I could be still so I could hear God. I would take any opportunity I could to sit in solitude this way together with this intelligent spirit and bask in its peace.

As you can imagine, all this was very different from the practice I was exposed to growing up. What parting your hair on one side of the head versus the other had to do with spirituality was a mystery to me. Does wearing make-up really make you a sinner? What seemed most important back then was that we made it appear as though we were living the perfect Christian life—whether we were really living that way or not. I could never reconcile those outer concerns and the importance of appearances with my inner, spiritual being.

I remember a day when I was around sixteen years old. My father told me it was time for me to decide whether or not to join the church. I told him straight out.

"Dad, I just can't do it."

He was supportive and didn't pressure me.

"Well, okay," he agreed. "Just as long as you go to church somewhere."

I promised him that I would and I kept my promise. I was so grateful for his answer and gained even more respect for him because of it. I loved my childhood and the strong sense of community in which I was raised. In hindsight, I can see that I was provided with a solid foundation for my ongoing spiritual growth as an adult.

I was taught as so many of us, that we are made in God's image. As an adult, finding my own spiritual life, I finally understood what this meant. We all have God's spirit within us. That's who we are. That's what we are. Pure spirit. Our human, physical bodies are simply an outer shell that houses the spirit that we've been given. Through this absolute knowing, I worked to completely surrender to this intelligent energy—to God—in all areas of my life. Doing this gave me peace and strength to deal with whatever I encountered each day. My philosophy became— just this day. No more.

Still, all this was easy to talk about in theory. It was certainly much harder to apply. How does any one human being stay connected and believe that life is unfolding just as it should—transform negative thoughts into positive ones—and see the blessing in disguise, when life itself becomes more than one can possibly bear? That day as we embarked on the journey to find Chris, it was time to put all that I had learned and practiced to the test. It was time to ride the currents of the river and search. It was time to handle just this day. No more.

Mary L. Cardin

Chapter Five

The Bridge

It was such a clear, beautiful day. I rode in the window seat of the rafting company's van to the river site. Looking out, I actually noticed the blue, cloudless sky. There was a stark contrast between the beauty of the day and the dark task lying ahead of us.

We rode in silence for most of the half-hour trip. Once we arrived at the place where we would put in at the river, the two guides, Joe and Ed, distributed our appropriate safety gear and gave us all the necessary safety instructions. Both guides expressed concerns once again about this trip, emphasizing the level of danger involved.

We put the rafts into the river approximately three miles north of the gorge bridge. A man was fishing on the east side of the river. There were only a few others nearby. On the opposite side of the river appeared to be a father, mother and their little son playing at the water's edge. It seemed like such a peaceful, surreal spot along the Rio Grande. It occurred to me that these folks were completely unaware of why our rafting group was going down the river today. To them, it must have looked like just another pleasure trip.

Just as the rafting company's owner had said, the water level was indeed quite low. I found myself questioning why a low water level presented more of a danger than it would if the water level was extremely high. But then again, I didn't know much about rafting. They certainly knew more about the river than I did, so I trusted them to safely take me down the river to look for Chris.

The guides assisted me as I put on an orange life jacket and helmet. They helped me into the raft and guided me to the middle seat. I had the seat to myself. Robert and

Ben were instructed to sit in front of me. Joe sat behind
me. I reached over the edge of the raft and put my fingers
down into the rippling, soothing water. I was grateful that
it was still warm on this 9th day of September. It had been
six long days since Chris was last seen or heard from.
Robert reached back and squeezed my hand, not saying a
word. His level of caring and his presence brought me
some comfort as we prepared to start down the river. I
knew, all the while, that his heart must be as heavy as
mine.

Robert seemed to have been a good friend to Chris,
even though they met just three months earlier in Taos.
They had a lot in common—artists, new in town, single and
probably lonely. Robert told me that he and Chris could sit
for hours, not say much, but then go away feeling like they
had engaged in a great conversation. It warmed my heart
to know that Chris had a good friend like Robert in Taos. I
was so grateful that Robert had decided to come down the
river that day and that he was in the raft with me. I needed
his stability and silent strength to help me through what I
was about to find.

Ed went solo in a separate raft so he could travel ahead of us to lead and scout the way. As the rest of us followed in the second raft with Joe as our guide, I saw Joe as an example of how God was putting the right people in my life at just the right time. Joe's spirit was so gentle and kind. His influence was exactly what I needed at this chaotic and emotional time.

As we pushed off to paddle down the river, I said underneath my breath,

"Please, Chris, if you're here, lead me to you."

My thoughts shifted as Joe began to give specific search directions.

"We need to be looking at every little piece of cloth and investigate every little reflection we see," Joe directed. "There are so many crevasses and rocks. We have to make sure we keep our eyes open for anything out of the ordinary. A body could be hidden anywhere."

And it was true. The crevasses between the rocks were huge and there were so many rocks. So many places a body could be. Small shrubbery grew out from between the rocky areas, hindering our vision. From above, the sides of the gorge didn't look so massive and deep, but from down in the river looking up, it all looked so overwhelming—too big. I couldn't imagine how we could ever find Chris if he *was* here.

I heard Ben's voice.

"Look, there are some mountain goats."

By then, we had gone approximately two and a half miles down the river from our entry point. At least six mountain goats were to the left side of our raft, standing on the edge of the rocks, looking interested as they peered down at us as we drifted past. I wondered how they managed to survive, living on the edges of such a sheer drop-off. The mama goats stood protectively beside their young. Any other time, this would have been a beautiful and exciting experience for me. It didn't feel beautiful or exciting today.

My eyes had been so focused on the sides of the gorge for three miles now, that I hadn't noticed that we were coming up on the bridge—the bridge from where Chris might have jumped—an overwhelming 650 feet above us.

Chris hated heights. Could he really jump from that bridge out into the blackness of the night? It didn't seem fathomable to me. That was what this trip was all about for me. I had to do my best to prove that he couldn't— that he didn't jump at all. I still held on to hope in spite of all that I knew.

As our rafts took us underneath the bridge, that nauseating feeling came over me again. But I told myself that I couldn't get sick. I had to stay strong. I focused on my silent request.

"Chris, if you're here, please lead me to you."

Joe chimed in with more guidance for us.

"Since we didn't find anything on the sides of the gorge upstream from the bridge, now we need to be looking in the water past the bridge."

This made sense to me. If Chris did jump and hit the water, his body would have been taken downstream somewhere. But I also remembered the police officer telling me that most folks that jump don't hit the water.

An eagle sat perched on the edge of a boulder on the west side of the gorge, to the right side of our raft. He remained still, looking down on us. It seemed that we all noticed it at the same time.

"Eagles never do that," Joe blurted out. I could hear the excitement in his voice. "They are known to always fly away even before you see them. This is amazing!"

Eagles had always been important to Chris. He felt that they spoke to his spirit and to him were symbolic of beauty, strength and freedom. Over the years, Chris had been commissioned several times to paint eagles and he loved doing it.

Joe had no idea of the impact that this information had on me in that moment. This majestic eagle examined us as we made our way down river. His beautiful golden head turned toward us, eyes following our every movement as we slipped by. Those eyes pierced through me, holding my gaze. Still, he didn't move. He didn't fly away. He seemed filled with wisdom, as if he was sent to guide us. He remained still, his full attention on me.

A few yards further downstream, a playful beaver on the left side of the river commanded our attention with his splashing and frolicking around a pile of wood in the shallow water. He noticed us, too, but then quickly disappeared into the water, sending gentle ripples toward our raft. The guide seemed to be astonished by all the wildlife present for us today along the river. He mentioned that this must be a sign of something. He wasn't sure what it meant, but he felt that it had to mean something.

"STOP!"

Ed, the solo guide in the lead raft, had begun to yell. And then I knew.

I just knew without anyone having to say anything else. My chest tightened. We had found Chris.

Joe directed us to steer our raft off to the right so we wouldn't move downstream any further. Joe also knew, but no one uttered a word until he and the others securely fastened our raft to the nearest rock.

"You stay here, Mary, and we'll go down to Ed and see what's happening," Joe said as he gently took my hand guiding me out of the raft. I sat down on the flat part of a huge rock along the river's edge. My eyes focused on my shoes and I wasn't sure if I could look downstream. But I knew I had to look. It was a forced effort to turn my head to the right and gaze toward the object Ed has seen in the water. Then I saw him. I saw Chris.

His partially naked body was lying face down in the water, stuck on some rocks, just yards down the river from where the eagle was perched and on the same side of the river. Chris had apparently hit the water and floated down river until the rocks at Yellow Branch Rapids caught him, just a little more than a mile south of the bridge. He did jump. He really did jump. Chris had actually killed himself.

In disbelief, all I could do was bury my head in my hands and sob openly.

"I'm so sorry. I'm so sorry", was all that I could say as my head became dizzy with the realization of what was true.

My new friends came over to me several times to try to console me, but there was no consoling to be done. So, for a while, as long as I needed, they let me be.

After some time, I managed to motion for Robert to come over to me. I asked him if he would please be the one to identify Chris' body, to make sure that it was Chris. I knew how hard this must be for Robert, but I also knew that there was no way I could do this myself. And I trusted Robert. Robert did identify the body and yes, it was Chris. Robert told me that Chris was shirtless, wearing a pair of shorts and one boot. One boot. His other boot had been back on that fence post. Chris had placed it there as his grave marker after all.

I wrapped my arms around my shaking body in an attempt to calm myself. Then I watched as Ed went over to Chris in the water. Ed bowed his head and said a prayer over Chris' body. I felt so touched by this. Ed's gesture will always remain etched in my heart and mind. He had brought a sense of peace to this horrific moment.

I didn't realize when we set out that morning that the place where we would find Chris' body would technically be considered a crime scene. Now the guides were telling me that we couldn't take Chris back with us. His body would be secured so it wouldn't float further downstream, but it would be the responsibility of the state police to come back for Chris.

I couldn't bear the thought of leaving Chris here after all this. All kinds of horrible images came to mind. What if the vultures *did* make their way to him tonight? It was only noontime and there were many daylight hours left for something else bad to happen to him. I begged the guides.

"Please, let me take him with us. Please."

But there was protocol to follow, and I had to accept that.

All of me wanted to wade through the water that stood between me and Chris and hold him against me again—to gently stroke his beautiful bald head and to tell him how much I loved him. Still, I stayed back and sat on that rock, dazed and weeping and trying to let the reality of it all sink in. Staying there, at a distance, was all I could handle. I knew that it was Chris in the water. I didn't have to see him any closer to know that it was him. And I kept telling myself that I also knew that this was just his body. And his body wasn't Chris. That I knew for certain.

Six very long days had passed since Chris had jumped. Like Mary Jo, ultimately I decided that I didn't want my last image of Chris to be a horrible one. He was a beautiful man and I wanted to keep that vision in my mind and remember instead the warmth of his body as we had hugged goodbye just a few months before.

After the guides finished their final preparations of securing Chris to the rocks and after they had given me sufficient time to feel up to the return trip, they walked over to where I was sitting. They gently took my hand so I could stand up and helped steady me. Their collective hug engulfed me with kindness. They offered up another prayer. This time, the prayer was for me.

I don't know where I found the strength to stand or to leave Chris behind. But I did. And I found the strength to pray.

"Please God, keep him safely untouched tonight. I don't want anything else bad to happen to him. Please God!"

As we pushed the raft back from the river's edge, I couldn't bring myself to look over at Chris' body again. I felt surrounded and protected by the new, dear friends traveling in the raft with me. When Joe handed me an oar,

I tried to get a good grip but it slipped out of my hands. I could barely hold it in place. My arms were too shaky and I was much too weak. I knew they would understand if I couldn't help with the rowing for the trip back. But I was determined. I grabbed the oar firmly the second time. I had to be strong.

I realized as we paddled out into the middle of the river and steered the raft toward the rapids that the only way down the river was to go past Chris' body. As we passed, weak with emotions, all I could do was whisper to him quietly and lovingly my final goodbye.

From that point in the river, we had about two and a half more hours to travel to arrive at a spot where we could exit the river. The exit point was near a little town called Pilar.

Numb, in shock, and finding it hard to breathe, the pain was unbearable. It was way past time for me to fall to pieces, but that luxury would have to wait until I helped my fellow rafters back down the river. Thoughts bombarded me with each stroke of the oar. What now? If Chris' life was over, my life was surely over, too.

After about an hour of rowing in silence, Joe asked me if I wanted to stop and have a bite of lunch. The guides had prepared sandwiches for us and were ready to find a nice grassy spot along the river bank where we could take a break. I was in a panic to continue on. I couldn't stop. I surely couldn't eat. I just needed to get to the end of this trip. I still had to tell Mary Jo that we found her brother. Everyone understood and we continued on down the river.

For the remainder of the trip I allowed the tears to fall freely and openly. I was thankful for the physical exercise of rowing. No one spoke much. What was there to say, really? We were all caught up in our own thoughts about Chris' death. Still, every once in a while, Robert would reach back and lovingly squeeze my hand or ask me if I was okay.

Eventually around 3:00 p.m., we finally neared the end of our journey. The rafting company van and trailer were parked at the ramp waiting for us. We were all physically and emotionally exhausted, but we managed to exit the river and load the rafts and equipment nonetheless. With the little strength that I had left, I gave each of my companions a huge hug and thanked them for all their efforts.

The task still remained to call the state police and inform them that we had found Chris. Robert volunteered to be the one to make that call. Once again, I was grateful for his stability and strength and thankful that he was with me that day. We rode back to the boat house in the van in total silence.

The quiet made a space for me to remember. The eagle. I knew the eagle had led me to Chris. A symbol of beauty, strength and freedom. All traits which belonged to Chris. And Chris had always valued his freedom most of all. And now, like the eagle, Chris was finally free.

Chapter Six

A Celebration of Life

As I pulled into the Sagebrush Inn parking lot, my emotions were uncontrollable. How could I find the words to tell Mary Jo that we had found Chris? I walked toward our room at the Inn and I saw that Mary Jo was waiting for me on the patio adjacent to our room. She took one look at me and she knew. Mary Jo knew that we had found her brother. For some reason, I felt I had to say it anyway, out loud for both of us to hear.

"We found Chris, Mary Jo."

We fell into each others' arms and wept. My husband, her brother, was dead. We held on tight to one another for what seemed like a long time. Neither of us could speak. Neither of us felt the need to speak. Our hearts, in total unison, were breaking.

After a while, my thoughts turned to Santana. Our sweet Santana. Chris' little boy. Mary Jo had brought him out to the patio with her on his leash. I gathered our little dog up into my arms and held him tight. Dogs know us. They feel what we feel. Santana knew that something had happened to his daddy. As I turned my face downward to look at him, Santana gently licked away my tears. I held our precious boy in my arms as Mary Jo and I settled into the plastic, white patio chairs to rest. I shared the details of our trip down the river and the events that led up to finding Chris' body.

Eventually, Mary Jo and I made the phone calls we had dreaded making. We delivered the unimaginable news to all the people we loved and who loved Chris. My sister Nancy and her husband Carl insisted on coming to Taos to be with me. I didn't argue. Later, Mary Jo and I decided to go down to the gallery to tell Lois. I told Mary Jo that I needed to shower first after the long river trip. In reality, a shower was my excuse to find a way to be alone with my grief.

Tears mixed with water as the shower washed over me. I was free once again to let the tears flow freely. They did. And through the tears I called out to Chris. Through the background noise of the shower spray, I heard myself whisper over and over again,

"Oh, Chris, I'm so sorry. I'm so, so sorry!"

―――――――――――――――

I was somewhat taken aback when we arrived at the gallery and shared the news with Lois. It was clear that she was not shocked or surprised. Lois said that several days after Chris went missing, she had a feeling that he had died. Lois told me that just three nights after Chris went missing, she woke up during the night and saw him lying in the other bed in her room. By the time she awakened her partner, Chris was gone. Lois said that it was at this point that she knew Chris was dead and that his spirit had come to see her that night. She didn't know for certain that he had jumped from the bridge. She *did* know, however, that Chris had died somehow and had crossed over.

In a strange, very small way, this information gave me some consolation. Both Lois and Sylvia had seen Chris in spirit. This meant that Chris was still with us and that his spirit was still alive.

Through my own spiritual evolution, I knew at some level that we could experience contact from those who had crossed over. This was just one more confirmation of this truth and it came at a time when I *needed* confirmation that it was true. We are spirits first and foremost.

Ben had been waiting for us back at the Inn. He joined me and Mary Jo in the lounge area and we ordered a round of drinks. Rum and Coke was Chris' standard drink of choice. So that's what we ordered. Rum and Coke all the way around. We sat there for hours and on into the night talking about Chris, the pain he must have been in and our pain of losing him.

Later that night, as I lay my head down on my pillow, the events of the day replayed like a movie over and over in my mind, preventing sleep from coming. I counted my blessings, too. Kay Borders, a very good friend of mine from Atlanta was flying to Taos to be with me. My brother Mel was driving over from Scottsdale. Mary Jo's husband, John and John's mother Judy were on their way. Chris' brother Ross and wife Debbie were headed my way from Arkansas. Chris' step-sister Kathy was flying in from Peru. Nancy and Carl would arrive the next day. It was so beautiful and overwhelming—the outpouring of love and kindness—all these wonderful people rallying to provide support.

Still, I struggled alone with that one heavy, unanswered question.

"Now what? What do I do now?"

As I lay there totally confused and exhausted, trying to sleep, Santana snuggled up under the covers beside me. My heart was breaking for Chris, for his pain, and I heard myself crying out to him all over again.

"I'm so sorry, Chris. I'm so, so sorry!"

More questions pounded in my head. Why did Chris end his life in this particular way? Why a bridge? But then, the answer came in the image of Chris' magnificent paintings. Just like any work of art Chris had ever created, there was symbolism here. A bridge leads the way from one place to another. A bridge can provide a way out. And the bridge was Chris' way to travel from this place to the next.

Morning finally did come, though in some ways I wished it never would. Not today. But I rose, knowing what to do next. I would plan a memorial gathering for the many folks in Taos that Chris had impacted and for those who were traveling so far to share their love and support. Chris had made so many friends in Taos. He was well-known in such a short time—the artist who painted at his easel in front of the Enchanted Dreams Foundation each day from eight o'clock in the morning until five o'clock at night. These wonderful friends to Chris and now to me and the sweet souls who Chris chose to spend his final days with must have a way to pay their respects to my husband, a beautiful man and magnificent artist. I knew the gallery would be a perfect setting for the gathering. Lois graciously agreed.

The day I began to plan Chris' memorial was also the day that the state police planned to retrieve Chris' body. They hired the same rafting company that took me down river. Joe and Ed would be their guides just as they had been mine. Officer Chandler and the medical investigator, Tamara Stephenson, would go along. Ed paddled solo again in the raft that would carry Chris' body. Chris was pronounced dead by Medical Examiner Stephenson on September 10, 2007, exactly one week after he took his life.

I stayed behind, but I may as well have been right there with them. I knew all the while that this gruesome task was happening at the gorge. I felt like I was smothering and drowning—gasping for air. I was forced to shut down my emotions for most of that day, just to stay alive. Moving forward with the gathering plans helped as much as anything could as Mary Jo and I pulled together the details. We were guided by our thoughts of what Chris would want us to do.

Chris would definitely want us to eat and drink—Mexican food—rum and Coke. He would want this to be a celebration rather than a memorial. The dress would be casual. Chris never much cared for stuffiness or formality. In some ways, I wasn't sure that Chris would have wanted a gathering at all—certainly not in his honor, but I felt that he understand that *we* needed it—I and all the folks who loved him needed this, too.

In the midst of planning, I recalled having seen Chris' Harley Davidson possessions in the back seat of his truck when the state police had returned the vehicle to me. Chris loved that Harley Davidson. So I decided to take his boots, vest, leather jacket and helmet with me to the gallery for the gathering. I planned to display the items on a chair underneath one of Chris' paintings. I needed to have as much of Chris around me as I possibly could. I needed to feel him there, helping me through this.

On Tuesday, Mary Jo and I met with the funeral director who would handle the cremation of Chris' body. Chris had told me that he wanted to be cremated many years before. I would honor his wish. The funeral director told me that he remembered seeing Chris painting in front of the gallery. He remembered how friendly and nice Chris had been.

It seemed to come as a shock to the funeral director that he would be cremating the body of a man he knew as a talented artist. The funeral director even helped Mary Jo and I put together a program to hand out at the gathering. I was touched by this personal gesture. A reporter from the local Taos newspaper came by to interview us as we worked on the program and took a photo. The photo and article appeared in the newspaper the following weekend.

The rest of the details for the gathering fell together easily. Mary Jo planned to write a letter to her brother and share her feelings with him at the gathering. She worked on putting the right words on paper for quite a while that day. Mary Jo and I also decided we would need to go shopping for something to wear for Chris' celebration of life. I had brought only one pair of old jeans and a tank top with me to Taos.

We found some good selections at a little local boutique. I decided on a pair of black jeans and a blue & black lacy blouse. It was not until I returned home to Durango, many days later, that I noticed the brand name tag on the jeans I wore to the gathering that marked the end of my husband's life on earth. They were tagged *Miss Me* jeans.

The Celebration of Life was held on Wednesday at the gallery that Chris so clearly loved and where he painted every day since his arrival in Taos. To open the celebration, I asked all the attendees to gather together in a circle and hold hands. We stood in the section of the gallery where Chris' art still hung on the walls. His art and his spirit surrounded us. I cradled Santana in my arms and held in the tears until later. I offered my gratitude to all who were there and I talked just a little about Chris and about the wonder of our life together. Then I provided an opportunity for the others to share a thought or a memory about Chris.

Mary Jo spoke first, reading verbatim the loving, touching letter that she had composed for her brother. Lois followed by reading one of her favorite scriptures. After each had shared their thoughts and stories about Chris, everyone stayed and mingled around the gallery. It was obvious that each in their own way wanted to be close to Chris' art and to his spirit for just a little longer.

The ceremony lasted nearly four hours. Another newspaper reporter, this one from the *Santa Fe North*, dropped by for an interview. *Wife Took Over Search* was the title of the article. It was published in the Sunday edition. It appears that the impact of Chris' death would be more far reaching than he ever might have imagined.

That night, following the celebration, a majority of us decided to have dinner at the Old Blinking Light north of Taos. The Old Blinking Light was another one of Chris' favorite area restaurants. We continued to honor Chris' life by sharing more memories of him. Some were humorous. Some were sad. Still, no matter the mood of the story, each was told with sweet and loving undertones. In an unexpected gesture of generosity and love, Mary Jo's mother-in-law, Judy, picked up the dinner tab.

On Thursday, when Mary Jo and I checked out of the hotel, the desk clerk informed us that my brothers and sisters had paid the entire bill. It was the outpouring of love and support that left me and Mary Jo standing at the checkout desk, holding each other and crying together once more—this time tears of gratitude. Unaware of our surroundings and not caring what anyone might think, we relaxed into this final tender moment together before going our separate ways. It was time for each of us to find our own roads to healing. This thing that had happened brought Mary Jo and I closer than ever, as so often happens in families during a crisis. We were truly sisters in spirit now. Our relationship and our lives were forever changed.

<u>Chapter Seven</u>

The Eagle Hunts Walking

My sister Nancy rode back to Durango with me. Her husband Carl followed, driving Chris' truck and carrying what was left of his belongings. When we arrived home from Taos, Carl and I unloaded Chris' stuff and all of his artwork. We carried everything into the house with a kind of reverence. For the time being, we set everything in the dining room.

When we were finished with the task, several boxes of personal items, two bags of clothing and two small overnight cases sat on the dining room floor. We set several boxes of lithographic prints of Chris' paintings on top of the dining room table. It would be weeks before I could even touch, let alone sort through, the pile that represented to me what was left of Chris' life. I looked around at what remained. This was all mine now and I couldn't even begin to consider what to do with all of the stuff or with the truck. These material possessions were all that I had left of Chris. Except for his ashes. I did have his ashes.

Chris' ashes had been placed in an ivory colored cardboard box. The box had a beautiful lacy pattern on the outside. As I carried the box inside that day, I held it close to me as if I could somehow be closer to Chris that way. I lovingly whispered to him,

"You're home again, Chris. You're home with me and Santana, where you belong."

I placed the box of ashes on a cabinet in my living room. I set up a memorial of sorts there—his glasses, his wallet and a candle with a photo of Chris attached to it given to me by the funeral home. As notes and sympathy cards came in, I placed them there, too, in a wooden box with a decorative handle. Eventually, I added some of my favorite photos of Chris and me in simple frames. This collection of things brought me such comfort. I needed Chris close by, where I could see him. I could see him there every time I walked into the room, every time I came in the front door of the old Victorian and every time I left. I needed to say good morning to him. I needed to tell him that I was home when I came in the door after work every day—just like we had done thousands of times, day after day during our life together.

When it was time for them to head home, Nancy and Carl had a hard time leaving me alone. But they had already stayed with me for three days, and it was time. I assured them that I would be fine, not at all sure that I would be. I was trying to convince myself as much as I was trying to convince Nancy and Carl that I could do this. I planned to go back to work soon and I had lots of good friends in Durango ready to provide support. I knew from my own experience with trauma in the workplace that the healthiest thing for me to do was to resume a normal routine as soon as possible. That was my plan.

So we hugged and I expressed my gratitude and love. Carl prayed over me. I couldn't imagine what I had ever done to deserve the love my sister and brother-in-law had shown through this ordeal. So I simply accepted their gift as one more confirmation that we are provided what we need in life at exactly the time that we need it the most.

Once on my own with no further distractions, the flow of tears did not stop for days. As I look back now, I'm not sure how I survived those initial days and weeks. The previous lessons I had learned about living in the moment helped a little, but this loss felt like more than my heart could possibly bear. I existed minute to minute. I ate little and cried much. I began to lose my *own* desire to live. Before Chris disappeared, I had just begun to process the emotional pain of our marital separation. Now it was time to face the fact that I had lost my husband forever. There would be no reconciliation. Did I really want to go on— alone?

My relationships with the wonderful elderly residents at the assisted living facility where I was employed helped me during working hours. I was able to take my focus away from myself and off of my own pain. I chose not to share my story and what I was going through with the residents there. I just soaked up the love and healing that they so naturally offered me on a daily basis and I gave love back. I had always felt that I received so much more than I gave in my work. I found myself so grateful that I had been guided into this profession. My work provided life saving healing, day after day.

My co-workers were amazingly supportive and kind. I sensed that they probably had no idea how much their love and support helped me in those initial weeks and months after Chris' death. But when my workday was over and I would walk back into my house, the loneliness consumed me. I didn't know what to do with myself. At times, I would just wander through the house and cry, like a lost child looking for something I knew I could never find. I would sit at the kitchen table for hours at a time, staring out the window, out onto the streets of Durango. It's as if I were watching the world go on without me. I knew I would never be the same. I wondered if the pain would ever go away. The emptiness was dark and deep. I was lost—and at the time, I had no desire to be found.

When my gaze would fall upon Chris' beautiful artwork, I felt gratitude to have his paintings back with me. I could still feel his passion. His talent and his genius still surrounded me. One by one, I began to hang Chris' art but the enchantment that once filled me by being surrounded by all this beauty paled now.

"Chris, I'm so, so sorry. Why did you do it?"

The overwhelming guilt and the still unanswered question of "why" held onto me and wouldn't let go. I needed an answer. I spent time feeling the level of pain and agony that I knew Chris must have felt in order to jump off that bridge. The question of "why" tormented me— followed me everywhere during my waking hours and into my dreams at night. It didn't help to know that Chris' deep wounds happened long before I came into his life. I was still haunted by the possibility that it was our separation that had sparked Chris' decision to end his life. There was no note—no message of explanation that could help me know for certain why Chris ultimately chose to leave this earth.

Was his decision to jump impulsive or had he planned this ending ever since we separated? Did he jump because he was lonely and missed me and Santana, or did he jump because he felt he had completed his life? At that moment, I could only guess. But I needed to know for sure.

Through my pain, I found myself hoping that I had been Chris' best love. I wanted to believe that in spite of the bumps in our relationship and his indiscretions that I was still his heart-mate, the one that he loved the most. He had always said that I was the best thing that ever happened to him. But was I, *really?* Now I might never know.

Somewhere in between the barrage of questions, I slowly found my way through Chris' belongings. In one of his black overnight cases, tucked away in one of the inner compartments, I found a trinket—a little dog made of clay with angel wings on it. It was his Santana angel. His love and his longing for us seemed at that moment confirmed. Thoughts of how much Chris loved and missed Santana made me feel selfish for keeping Santana with me, even though I felt it was the right thing to do at the time. I fell to my knees, held the little clay dog to my chest and cried out,

"I'm so sorry, Chris."

The little clay dog would be placed with all the other memorabilia that I kept nearby as a reminder of Chris.

Sleep didn't come easily during this period of time, when it came at all. Most nights I would just lie in bed feeling heavy. I called out for Chris and begged his spirit to come to me. Then, finally, on one particular night about two months after his death, Chris came.

He came to me in a dream. In the dream, Chris and a friend had been golfing. Afterward, they came to our house for dinner. I remember thinking,

"But you're dead. You can't be home for dinner."

Next, as scenes change so quickly in a dream, Chris and I were in a room, sitting side-by-side. Two men in uniforms were sitting at their desks across from us. They reminded Chris that he was dead. Chris was seated next to me. He got up from his chair and walked toward one of the men. Chris lifted his golf cap and began to speak. Just two words.

"Now listen..."

The dream was over.

A wave of physical energy jolted me awake. It was such a strong sensation that I felt it throughout my body. My heart was pounding. I knew in that moment that Chris' spirit was moving through me.

I settled into the experience feeling grief and gratitude at the same time. This was my first dream of Chris since his death. I knew with certainty that this was a visit and though I was thankful, it was not enough. I wanted more of him. But for now, I would have to be satisfied with this short, bittersweet reunion.

I always saw Chris as not only talented and intelligent, but as the most big-hearted person I had ever met. Chris' kind and generous nature was confirmed many times over in the weeks following his death as the cards, notes, phone calls and email condolences began to pile in. So many of these communications were sent to testify to Chris' generosity.

Chris liked having nice things, but money and material things never motivated him. He would always give freely whenever he saw a need. I received touching accounts from every direction about Chris and his kind, giving nature and his huge heart. Chris was a man who would do what needed to be done whether someone needed money, a ride, or a favor.

I found one story particularly heartwarming. It came from a local preacher in Taos. He and Chris had coffee together most mornings at a local coffee shop. Chris had never asked what his coffee partner did for a living but during their last conversation together, he *did* ask. When Chris heard that the guy was a preacher, his response was one of surprise as he said,

"Get out of here! Really?"

The preacher had an unconventional look about him as preachers go, with long braided hair and casual attire. During that last visit, the preacher shared with Chris his dream of opening a shelter for homeless men in Taos. The preacher said that Chris didn't miss a beat as he opened his wallet and handed him a pile of bills saying

"Let me be your first donor."

When Chris moved out of our house and headed west, he had close to $13,000 in cash with him. When he died, only that $27 I found in his wallet was left. That story of giving led me to believe that Chris knew his ultimate intention to leave this world well in advance and had given the money away as one of his final gifts.

The stories and notes gave me comfort at times and at other times unearthed more heartache and confusion for me. I so deeply loved Chris. His family loved him. He was admired by so many. Why wasn't that enough? I knew all those years that Chris' emotional scars ran so very deep. I accepted that Chris had loved me as best he could and as fully as he was capable of.

Mary L. Cardin

Eventually, I ran across a poem that Chris had written many years before. The title was, *The Eagle Hunts Walking.* I remembered the eagle at the river that had led us to Chris. Though I would certainly continue my search for answers and for a way to find peace in all the questions, the words that Chris had poured out of his heart and into this poetry brought some solace in the present moment. His words weaved a sort of comfort through my pain. Between the lines, I found a first step onto my path of understanding.

> *The Eagle Hunts Walking, who's wounded his wing*
> *To fall from the clouds, a transitional thing.*
>
> *He soared on the wind, the proud and the free*
> *From his place in the sun, all things he could see.*
>
> *His power was great, of beauty and truth.*
> *Now he is hungry, alone and aloof.*
>
> *The great teacher of life has shown him the way.*
> *A hunter is hunted, the predator, prey.*
>
> *To feed with the crows at twilight's last gleaming*

What happened to life, so gallantly streaming?

The Eagle Hunts Walking and freedom has flown.
Security's promise, as cold as a stone.

To live among wolves, the price of the life.
In liberty's absence, you run fast, or die.

~ Chris Cardin

Mary L. Cardin

<u>Chapter Eight</u>

My Grief Journey

Everyone experiences grief in their own unique way. No one way is right, and no one way is wrong. What *is* imperative for everyone is that they must experience, feel and work *through* the grief and sorrow or they run the risk of being stuck in it for the rest of their lives.

So perhaps out of my fear of being stuck in this dark and painful place, I ate healthy foods when I didn't feel hungry. I avoided making major decisions for a while. I chose not to be angry at Chris but not to romanticize our relationship either. I kept myself reminded that even if

Chris had lived, I had chosen to live my life without him. I didn't dwell on the past but I had to force myself to remember what was true. Most of all, I didn't think much about the future because the future seemed so far away. I focused on today and made it through one day at a time.

Initially after Chris' death, it was hard for me to read, especially any material that had anything to do with God. Eventually, I forced myself to read a little something each day, whether I absorbed any of it or not. I began with a daily devotional that one of my sweet nieces had sent me entitled *Streams in the Desert*. The daily inspirational messages seemed to speak directly to me. The words eased the pain just a little as I read each day. Slowly, I added grief-related titles and booklets for survivors of suicide to my reading list.

I had always been taught that all things work for good for those who love God. It was hard for me to believe in *that* concept during this time. I wasn't even able to pray. I wasn't angry with God, as some say they experience during a time of loss. But I was lost and couldn't find my spiritual path again or any real meaning in my life.

I had read things about how we need to hold on and to trust God through tough times. Hold onto what? I wanted so badly to get back on some spiritual path. Why did I feel selfish wanting that now? I found a counselor. She told me I could never get back on the same spiritual path again. She said I had been given a new path. Working through this experience *was* my path, my journey now.

The counselor recommended that I meet with a grief support group. She referred me to two local group leaders. I was willing to try anything and everything in order to work through the grief and pain I was feeling.

It remained difficult for my out-of-state family to be so far away. They continually expressed how helpless they felt as I went through this trauma alone. Still, they found ways to be with me even from far away. And in yet another amazing gesture of love and support, they came together to pay for my individual therapy sessions as a healing gift. Weekly sessions helped me find the strength and the courage to make it from one week to the next—from one session to the next. And in between, I was able to continue living.

My counselor's office was next door to a Kairos Therapist, a form of energy healing therapy. My counselor was aware of the physical symptoms I was experiencing since Chris' death and suggested that I might find this form of therapy helpful. I followed her recommendation. I benefited so greatly from Kairos Therapy that I signed up for a succession of eight sessions. The theory behind the sessions was to help me release the negative energy that I was storing in my body, deep within my cells. The Kairos Therapist explained that I was carrying most of my sadness and pain in my upper neck and head area. I was also holding a lot of my painful emotions in the joints of my hands. After a few months of Kairos Therapy, my severe neck and joint pain began to resolve.

Also, I signed on with a ten-week grief therapy group as my counselor recommended. At the time, I felt that a suicide survivor group might be more beneficial to me, but there was no such group in my immediate area. I was still struggling with the why of Chris' suicide and the guilt of whether he may have jumped as a direct response to my asking for a separation. Why hadn't Chris given me more time—time to call him back when I was ready to see him? It was hard for me to believe that Chris would have come to see us to say a final goodbye if he knew suicide was his intent and his sole purpose was to say goodbye. What would have happened if I had allowed him to come to see us when he called? I needed to know—or I needed to *stop* needing to know.

I began to feel that, buried in my own grief, I may be holding Chris back from his next spirit life—a life I wanted to be beautiful and joyful for him. I knew that I would eventually need to release Chris for his sake—and for mine but I didn't feel ready. Then one night, I woke up knowing that I had to try to let him go. I didn't want him to suffer anymore.

So that night, in the dark, I slowly drifted down the long flight of stairs from my bedroom to the living room. Amidst the shadows, I found the box of ashes and placed my hands on either side. I spoke to Chris as if he were right there listening to every word. In that moment, somehow I knew that he was. I told Chris how much I still loved him— that I loved him so much that I couldn't let my grief tether him to the earth plane from which he so longed to escape. I thanked him for being in my life. I apologized for all the hurts I had caused him. I thanked him for his visit and invited him to come back to check on me and Santana whenever he felt he could. I wished Chris a new life filled with love, blessings and peace.

Then, feeling as if Chris' beautiful spirit was nestled gently in the palms of my hands, I walked outside and carefully lifted my arms upward towards the heavens and released him into the cool, gentle night. In that instant, I knew that Chris was gone. My life without him and the end of *us* had begun. I felt his absence like I had never felt it before. I sank down cross-legged onto the cold, damp ground, put my face on my hands, and wept.

Later, back inside, even amidst the lost feelings and surrounded by what felt like the shadow of death, I experienced a new beginning, too. As if God was leading me—as though my life had a plan, even though at this moment, I had no idea what that plan might be. I felt hope for a fleeting moment but then the hope quickly gave in to desperation all over again. There would be more letting go to come.

I crawled back into bed. I let the night sounds that came through my open bedroom window comfort me. I thought that I would feel better after this ritual. Instead, the pain in my heart was deeply physical and had intensified to the point that the agony prevented sleep. Chris was free now. Free to soar. I imagined him soaring like an eagle—like the eagle along the Rio Grande River. His spirit would always "be." The tears continued to flow and the pain built up to a new crescendo. I felt alone, abandoned and left behind.

The events over the past year had taught me that I was not in control. I had always tried to control my future, make the plans, but now things weren't turning out at all as I had planned. That night was the beginning of my learning to let go. But it was *only* the beginning.

My Lord God, I have no idea where I am going. I do not see the road ahead of me. I cannot know for certain where it will end. Nor do I really know myself, and the fact that I think that I am following your will does not mean that I am actually doing so. But I believe that the desire to please you does in fact please you. And I hope I have that desire in all that I am doing. I hope that I will never do anything apart from that desire. And I know that if I do this you will lead me by the right road though I may know nothing about it. Therefore will I trust you always though I may seem to be lost and in the shadow of death. I will not fear, for you are ever with me, and you will never leave me to face my perils alone."

~Thomas Merton

My niece sent me this prayer. The words not only helped me, they prepared me. That night, I asked God to send me a clear message. I needed some idea of where I was going. My prayer was answered with more-than-a dream-come-true.

Chapter Nine

The Adobe

From an early age, I always dreamed of living out west in a southwestern-style adobe house. I would find that house. But it would become more than that. It would be my healing sanctuary and a true gift from God—the answer to my prayer.

Not long after I had released Chris, I was invited to attend a sound-healing seminar that was being held at this particular adobe house. I decided to go. My initial impression when I walked in to the place was,

"WOW!"

If this had been my home, it would definitely have been my more-than-dream-come-true. The three-story house was a stunning combination of deep terra-cotta colored stucco with bright turquoise trim. It sat regally on a hilltop with a front yard with a strategically designed wildflower garden. I have always had a passion for flowers. My mother shared that passion with me. She always tended a lush flower garden as I was growing up. So being welcomed by a garden gave me an immediate feeling of being at home.

I was taken on a tour of the adobe house and guided through each spectacular room with its Mexican tile floors, massive wood-beamed ceilings and windows that took up the entire east wall on every floor of the house. The views overlooking the town of Durango were breathtaking. At the time, I wondered whether I could ever be comfortable living in such a large, beautifully-customized house. I wasn't sure if I deserved such luxury without Chris here to share it with.

The healing seminar at the house was helpful, and after that evening, I went back to focusing on my work and my grief recovery process. Several months later, thoughts of the house returned and I just couldn't get that place out of my mind. So much so, that I called the friend who had invited me to the seminar and knew the owners. I asked her if she thought the owners might consider selling their adobe house. Her answer marked the beginning of my miracle.

"They just decided to put the house on the market yesterday."

Immediately, I arranged for a private showing since I was told that a contract had not yet been signed with a real estate agent. The owners gave me their price and their terms. They allowed one week for me to decide whether I wanted to buy the place. I must admit, I was a bit overwhelmed by the overall size of the house and by the price tag. I thought it through and when the week was up, I called the owners and declined. I just didn't feel at peace with such an undertaking. Not yet.

Just three days later, the owners of the adobe called me back and wanted to negotiate further. They still felt the house was meant for me. I agreed to meet with them. After more discussion, I declined for a second time. The financial obligation was still more than I was willing to accept. But the owners were right. This was my house. I knew it, too. The house would provide the foundation for my new life. It represented forward momentum and healing.

On my spiritual journey, I had come to understand that we all have the power to create our own realities. It's all about faith. Ask and you shall receive, right? God said if we have the faith of a mustard seed, we can move mountains. As I took more and more responsibility for healing my personal grief, I began to build a new level of true faith. I knew that if we truly have faith when we deeply desire something, we shall receive. I knew that hoping was not enough. True faith was the key. I would have to apply this sort of certainty now.

So I surrounded myself with thoughts of what I wanted. I began to expect that good things in life would come to me. They would come not because I had suffered so much that I deserved more than anyone else, but because it was through the pain and loss that I had evolved into a woman who could tap into spirit and then attract and manifest my desire. So I let go. I visualized. And each time a thought of the house came into my mind, I would simply say,

"Thy will be done."

Three short months after I declined to buy the house for the second time, the owners contacted me. The house had not yet sold. They asked if I would I consider leasing the home with an option to buy. They stated their terms and gave me a week to decide.

As the week sped by, I still couldn't find clarity on what to do. Amidst the emotions of grief, loss and monumental life changes, clarity is often inaccessible. I really wanted this house, but I was also quite comfortable staying where I was. At that point, I wanted to be where God intended for me to be. On the day before I was required to make my decision, I went into my study to meditate and for the specific purpose of seeking spiritual guidance on what I should do. I expected an answer. I was certain.

It was a sunny day. The light beamed through the study window as I lay down on the futon, trying to clear my mind. Every time a thought of the house came to me, I repeated those same words.

"Thy will be done."

I'm not sure how long I lay there in a meditative state, but suddenly the message came through. I saw a vision of Chris' artwork hanging on the walls of that beautiful adobe house and I heard these words loud and clear,

"This house is a perfect showcase for Chris' art."

Chris and I had always planned on coming west to open a gallery for his art. Now I knew I had to move forward with that dream alone—and in the adobe house. It would be the perfect setting for private showings. I became so excited about the message that I jumped up and immediately called the owners and told them that I would sign a lease. I would be allowed to live in the house for one year before moving forward with a possible purchase, an arrangement that was a perfect compromise for me.

Just thirteen short months after arriving in Durango, I was ready to move into my more-than-my-dream-come-true-adobe home. God and the universe had given me the desire of my heart. The adobe house would be mine. Not because I hoped for it or because I allowed thoughts of it to consume me but because I let go. But why did I have to be there without Chris? What about *that* desire? My desire for *him*? Chris had always said that he shared the dream of moving west and together showcasing his artwork. But I understood now that Chris had chosen another path. Now the adobe house represented a new beginning for me and the ability to continue Chris' legacy.

Still, there was more to it than that. The adobe house and the progression of synchronistic events that made it my home had renewed my faith in my own spiritual process. This was no ordinary house. It was a healing sanctuary. Just as the owners had hosted healing seminars there, the house, its rooms and its walls would breathe new life into me, and give healing life to each of

Chris' healing gifts of art. Within the walls of the adobe house, my life again could find structure, strength, and I would be protected. And everyone who came through its doors would feel its energy and take a part of that wonderful energy with them to share with others. Through that house, the spirit of Chris, his art and his love for his Native people would join with my own spirit and we could reveal more light for others than either of us could have revealed alone. We would redefine the purpose for which Chris and I had been brought together in this life.

Now it was time to pack, sort, get rid of a lot more stuff and it was time to let go of a part of my past. Once I had completed all that work, I gathered together my wonderful friends and they helped me move—forward.

Chapter Ten

Molly's Tears

Letting go came in small steps. Just when I thought I had let go, I would discover I hadn't—not really. Two years had passed since that phone call from Officer Gallegos. Everything in my life was new. I was tapping into my deep faith in order to make my dreams come true and in so many ways, what I was doing was working.

Here I was, living out west in a beautiful adobe house. I was hosting shows in order to share the energy of Chris' art with the public. I was surrounded by loyal friendships with remarkable women and I led an active social lifestyle—weekly girls' night out, happy hour, dinner parties, concerts, hiking, and biking through the scenic trails of beautiful Durango, Colorado. My work with the elderly still filled my soul and I knew I made a difference for these wonderful folks every day. Along the way, I had attracted a loving, healthy, spiritual relationship with a very special man into my life. To the outside world, I was healed and my dreams had come true.

Every morning, I woke up, gazed out of the wall of windows in my bedroom that overlooks a peaceful little town and gave thanks. Every night, I went to sleep giving thanks.

Still, with all the healing and amidst my shiny new life, there were ashes. The decorative ivory box, the candle and all our pictures had moved with me to the adobe house. The wooden basket of sympathy cards and notes were all still there. The little clay angel dog sat there, too, as the centerpiece. This time I set up the memorial items in my home office atop a cedar chest that once belonged to my mother. I had discarded Chris' glasses and wallet but the other memorabilia remained. Chris' death had come and gone and I knew he had in many ways, moved on to his new life, too. But there was yet another step to my releasing him—and to allow him to release me. What would I do with his ashes? From within my dream come true, I agonized. I asked Chris. A month later, I woke up one morning knowing what to do.

It was at the Rio Grande Gorge in Taos, New Mexico, where Chris had chosen to end his life. At that moment, Chris had chosen his final resting place. But then again, the thought of Helen, Georgia, kept infiltrating my messages, too. Divine timing took over and my friend Kay from Atlanta called and said she was coming to Durango for a visit. Kay and I had a delightful time together. Then, on the morning of Kay's planned departure back to Atlanta, I got out of bed earlier than usual—even before the sun came up. I had bought a little leather pouch for today and I took it with me along with the box containing Chris' ashes. I drew Chris close to me and, wrapped in a blanket, together we made our way up the stairs to my rooftop terrace.

Stretching out in a lounge chair, I held my precious Chris next to my heart. We kept one another warm in the chilled morning air and watched the sun come up. When the sun finally showed its face, I lifted the lid of the box that after two years, still looked like new. I slowly opened the plastic bag sitting inside the box that kept the ashes from spilling. I imagined Chris' spirit making its way to freedom. I symbolically released him. Once more, I told him that now he was free. The love in my heart came through in my voice as I explained that I was letting him go, this time for sure and this time for good.

I carefully scooped a tiny portion of Chris' ashes into the little leather pouch. Kay would take the little pouch back home with her and make a special trip to Helen to release just this little bit of Chris' spirit into the place that he loved so very much.

On a Saturday morning several days after Kay's departure, I drove to Taos with Chris' ashes riding on the passenger seat and Santana once again on my lap. I went alone. This final ending would be a private moment just between me, Chris and God.

A year before, to commemorate the anniversary of Chris' death, I had also returned to the gorge bridge in

Taos, at that time accompanied by Mary Jo and Kay. I had hired the same rafting company to take us back down the river. Joe was once again my guide on the river trip that marked the one year anniversary.

That trip was fairly uneventful. There was not as much wildlife as the previous year, but it was beautiful and sweet nonetheless. I again found it difficult to go underneath the bridge, then with the certain knowledge that Chris had jumped from that very spot. When we were directly under the bridge, I found myself in a visualization of exactly how he might have landed, and precisely where he might have hit in the water after plummeting from 650 feet above us.

It had been a difficult task to stop at the Yellow Branch Rapids, the rapids where Chris' body had been caught up. But we did stop. I wanted Mary Jo and Kay to know exactly where we had found Chris. We spent time there, toasted to Chris with rum and Coke and as a final gesture, tossed some of the drink mixture into the river, a token for Chris. We paused along the way for the gourmet picnic lunch I had missed the year before.

During that anniversary trip, I was somewhat able to enjoy the beauty of the surroundings. I enjoyed the dangerous rapids, the hard work of rowing, and the thrill of being tossed into the water once or twice. Then, a year later, I noticed that the beauty of the place came even more clearly into view.

With that second return to the gorge, I prepared myself for a new level of letting go. I replaced my sandals with a pair of comfortable sneakers, checked to be sure I had my cell phone with me in case of emergency and grabbed the box of ashes and a bottled water. I walked toward the gorge's west rim trail entrance. A few visitors and hikers hung around the area nearby but as I made my way further down the trail, I was relieved to be in solitude. I hiked the west rim trail for a mile or so, noticing myself holding on to the box of ashes just a little too tight. I talked to Chris the entire time. And as we neared our destination, I asked Chris to give me a sign that he was pleased with what I was doing that day.

A wooden bench near the edge of the gorge rim provided a resting place and a view down into the river and the Yellow Branch Rapids below. I was headed for those rapids—the place where we had found Chris. I sat on the bench, still talking to Chris and reliving the events of the previous two years. I clung tighter now to the box and that made me wonder if I was really ready to leave him here. It was final. I would have to part with him. This time, I was really letting him go—forever. Once I spread his ashes there, I thought Chris wouldn't be with me anymore. I felt I would be leaving all of him behind.

I moved forward, for my sake and for Chris. I got up from the bench, walked a few yards down the gorge and found a flat rock on the very edge of the gorge rim—a perfect place to sit. It felt warm from the September sun. It felt dangerous and risky to sit so close to the edge. I visualized how easily it would be to slip and fall headlong into the gorge below. Still, I wanted to be as near to the edge as I could be. Was it just because I wanted to ensure that Chris' ashes would go into the river below and float down stream as I had planned? Or was there more to it than that?

Sitting on the rock and enjoying the warm sun on my back, I opened the box and the bag inside. I didn't think to bring something for scooping the ashes out of the bag. Now I realized my hand would have to do. With each handful of ash, a new feeling ran through me. Some thoughts were mournful, others eerie. This was all that was left of him. This would be the last time I would hold him and his love in the palm of my hand.

I gently tossed each handful of ash down toward the gorge and the wind gently delivered Chris back to the river, handful by handful. I might have planned some ceremonial mantra, but all I could say now was,

"Be free, my love, be free."

I hesitated a long time before releasing the last handful of ash. Then, I just sat there, in a sort of trance. Suddenly, I had the need to hear his voice. The need was overwhelming. I reached for my cell phone, remembering that I still had a saved recorded message that Chris had left for me a while back. I dialed up my voice mail and placed the phone to my ear, listening to his husky voice and to the last words he ever said to me.

I listened to the message just once. A few months later, I would find the courage to delete the message.

I closed the cell phone, just in time. I looked up and a wave of peace and happiness flooded through me. There it was. My sign. My eagle.

He soared as if just for me, to the bridge then turned in flight and headed back south and into the gorge. I was sad that my eagle was gone, the experience and that magnificent connection to Chris had ended. But then he returned, raising my spirits and my hopes once again as he continued to perform for me—graceful, strong and majestic. Before he left me once more, my eagle flew directly over my head, flapped its wings one perfect time, and then he disappeared south into the gorge.

I cried through my words of gratitude,

"Thank you, Chris. I love you."

I was now ready to walk out of the gorge and into a new life. Both my body and my heart felt much lighter than when I walked in. I knew that I would be fine and that Chris was fine now, too.

I understood, too, in that moment, that it would be a long time before my tears – Molly's tears—would stop. And I was right. Molly's tears would continue to flow as a way to cleanse my soul and in remembrance of my beloved Christopher Lyle Cardin.

Chapter Eleven

Peace, My Final Gift

In 2007, a few days after I had arrived in Taos to look for Chris, Lois said she had something special to show me. She presented me with two original paintings. I knew immediately that this was Chris' work. The colors, the style, the intensity, the passion, and the detail of the faces of the Native American subjects were all signatures of his fine work. But these were exceptionally beautiful. Chris had painted his finest in these last two works of art.

One was a blue-colored painting depicting a native woman, tilting her head slightly to the right, her hand outstretched, holding a butterfly. Butterflies—the symbol of transformation. The woman in the painting was so beautiful and looked so peaceful. Her spirit drew me right in to the canvas. Chris primarily painted male figures, so I wondered who she might be. It had been so long since Chris had painted a woman, so I knew that there was significance to this particular work. I never have discovered its meaning. Lois had explained that this was Chris' next to last painting. The one with the circle, she told me, was his last.

His last painting. These words sliced like a dagger into my heart.

Then I saw it. His last painting. Magnificent colors of orange, yellow, red and purple. A proud native warrior in the center of the canvas with a circle around him. His hands stretched forward offering a peace pipe. I wasn't sure if it was earth or sky surrounding him, but the landscape parted. At first, I thought that this opening might represent the gorge. After another look, I felt as if I was watching the heavens part behind the handsome native figure.

Chris was intense and deep with his thinking process. I knew that there was always great meaning behind every single stroke of his paint brush. This piece was so proud, so peaceful, and the colors so vibrant. It would only be after I hung this final work in my adobe dream home in Durango, Colorado, and I was healed enough and open enough that I could receive the messages that this amazing final work was meant to convey. Chris' spirit delivered this information to me through a visit to his sister, Mary Jo. Below is the meaning of this fine work— what Chris would say if he could tell us in his own words what he so wanted us to understand.

The name of my last painting is Peace, My Final Gift. *It depicts my desire to enter a new life in the spiritual world. I am that warrior holding the peace pipe, the Chanupa, in my hands. The bowl of the Chanupa is filled with the bark of a red dogwood. When the Chanupa is smoked, the spirit of peace through prayer will drift up to the Great Spirit to make the prayer hold.*

The seven claws around my neck are bear claws. They represent the seven sacred rights of the Lakota. I have the honor to wear these seven claws because I am now the Wisdom Keeper—the keeper of seven directions and Mother Earth, Sky, Wind, and Water. The one feather near the bowl of the Chanupa represents a young man's life and the fringe represents what has been done in that life.

By worldly standards, I was still a young man when I decided to leave the earth. From the feather and the fringe on the stem of the Chanupa, other beings will know what band I am from and how experienced I am as a warrior. The three feathers on the right side of my head were received in combat and the one feather on the left, because it is hanging downward, tells you that I was at peace at one time in my life.

With my hands out-stretched holding the Chanupa, I offer peace to the Great Spirit before I am able to leave this earth and enter the world of spirit. A warrior must meditate, study, cleanse his own spirit of any past negative forces, and observe for one year before he can go to the Spirit World as a spirit himself. A warrior must prove to the great spirit that he is ready to leave the earth and leave behind all of his worldly possessions, his self-doubt, his self-hated, envy, jealously, and all other negativity that will get in the way of his eternal and external peace.

The circle surrounding me is an aura of peace leading me to the sky—this provides an opening in the sky for me to enter and present the Great Spirit with the Chanupa, its smoke and its peace. When the bowl containing the bark of the red dogwood was lit, the smoke created a circle around me, the Warrior.

From within this painting, I hand you the Chanupa—the same gift of peace that I offer to the Great Spirit. I am asking you to be at peace with living the life of the person you are meant to be—the soul you want to be. Be true to yourself and in doing so, be at peace with the decision to honor yourself and not the ones who try to stifle you.

When I chose Taos as my new home, I chose it because I knew I would discover and have the courage to live a simple life where I could meet people with similar desires, dreams, goals and beliefs. I needed to create a new life where I could let go of material possessions. There, I won my final struggles with demons old and new. Once I reached the water, I could no longer feel my past life. Once I made it to the other side, I was able to shed my fear, shame, sadness, jealously, and all of my other weaknesses. I took my shame with me when I jumped from the bridge then released it. Then, in peace, with the eagle beside me, I flew away.

After I received this powerful and insightful message, I made the conscious decision to accept Chris' gift—his final gift of peace. Chris was at peace with his life, his healing and his decision to move on. It was time for me to be at peace, too—with my life, with my healing, and with my decision to move on—without him.

<u>Chapter Twelve</u>

Moving On

Before we can move forward, we must let go of the past. I had a handle on this concept in theory, but what does it really mean to let go of the past? Letting go of the past for me meant to untether myself but not detach myself. I would need to stop any hanging-on that would keep me connected to a part of my past in such a way that it negatively impacted my life in the present and my ability to create the future of my dreams.

Writing the first chapter of this book began the process of my final letting go. But it would be in writing this final chapter that I would truly set the foundation for moving on into my miraculous new life.

The core process that had driven my spiritual growth and my profound healing has been much like planting a tree. It all begins with a seed. The seed, in my case was always a thought. Beginning my spiritual journey, asking Chris to leave, moving to Durango, finding my more-than-dream-come-true adobe house and all the steps I took to letting go of Chris all began with a thought.

Then, the thought became a desire. The desire is like the planting of the seed. It represents all the exciting possibilities to come and so the desire to "become" builds and builds until something must be done. Some action must be taken, and nothing on a small scale will do. The action ensures that the seed is watered and fertilized and tended.

With each step, I realized, there was an action that I took before letting go. I acted when I asked Chris to leave, the hardest thing I had ever done. I acted when I leased the adobe house, a real stretch for me financially. It's after we take the action that the concept of letting go comes in. At that point, we have done all that we can humanly do. It's time to invite God and the Universe—a Great Spirit to join with us to fully manifest the dream. The dream is the fruit that comes to us as a result of the initial seed we planted with just a thought.

As I watched this process unfold for me, I could only wonder if this was Chris' process, too, when he decided to end his life. That seed of thought may have come to him even before his indiscretion in Atlanta. Perhaps he knew that betraying me was the first extreme action he must take to manifest his ultimate freedom. I'll never in this life know for sure what was true for him. But I still wonder.

As I pondered the potential content of this last chapter, I looked around the adobe house and my eyes rested on the shrine-like memorial that I had carried around throughout my healing process. Chris' picture looked back at me and his eyes planted the thought. It was time to tear down this tribute. I would never forget. I would still give myself permission to cry sometimes. But this was the last step to moving on for both me and Chris. I let the desire build. It took weeks, but finally my desire to move forward in my life once and for all overcame my desire for the false comfort of the material things that the shrine represented.

I wrote this book for one purpose. I needed to share my experience with others in hopes that my journey and my steps to healing would give others hope, comfort, and a practical way to get through paralyzing pain and grief. My desire to share and to help others heal took root. I would need to take a courageous action. I would dismantle the shrine. This material representation contained the energy of Chris and the energy of holding on for both of us. Together we had let go in stages over the past 4 years. Now it was time to let go of an energy that was holding us back.

So on the evening of Monday, April 9th, 2012, with the resolve of creating the right final chapter for this book, I took my first step in the dismantling process. I surrounded myself with music by one of Chris' favorite artists, Robin Miller. The piece was called *Transcendence*.

I had no idea how much fear, dread and deep sadness remained and the resolve it would take for this final step but I knew the timing was right.

I visualized Chris' energy being slowly released as I removed pictures from frames. I allowed myself one final look at each paper memory; a custom-built Harley; our house in Atlanta; together on our 20th anniversary cruise and side by side at my niece, Tonya's wedding. I moved the little clay angel dog to its more proper place, among all the other Chihuahua souvenirs in my bedroom.

I cradled the candle that held Chris' picture on the outside in my palms. I knew with it, I held a bit of Chris' sweet, loving, generous spirit. I needed to enjoy that sense of him for just a bit longer and as I did I re-read the poem along side his picture.

"I'd like the memory of me to be a happy one. I'd like to leave an afterglow of smiles when life is done. I'd like to leave an echo whispering softly down the ways, of happy times and laughing times and bright and sunny

days. *I'd like the tears of those who grieve to dry before the sun of happy memories that I leave when life is done."*

I had gone as far as I could go with the dismantling process for that night. So I went to bed and resumed in the morning, dwelling on those happy memories. I would keep the candle. Not to hold me back, but to help me move forward with those happy memories whenever I needed to, maybe on special occasions, but especially on days like today.

I lit the candle and continued the process. The box that had once held Chris' ashes was now filled with notes and sympathy cards. I sat with the box on my lap for quite a while, stroking it gently, feeling the texture of its ivory colored paper covering through the tips of my fingers. I reread each expression of love and concern. The words were hard to hear and the strong emotions of others hard to navigate. My own pain rose to the surface, both emotional and physical and the tears arrived in time to begin a final cleansing. I had to stop every few minutes and take a break, but I was determined to push through since freedom for me and for Chris and perhaps for others would be the ultimate reward.

I kept reading. A poem from our niece, Julie:

A Very Private War

Deep was his pain, it cut him to the core. I didn't know he was fighting that strong internal war.
The battle in his mind was more than he could stand. He would not share his trouble. He was a very private man.
It wore him down. We could not see till he took the life of his own worst enemy.

A poem written by another friend of Chris' from Taos, Jim McBrayer:

In Memory of Chris

Chris, why did you leave so soon? Such a magnificent soul. Primal dreams set to canvas. Passion behind artist's eyes. Your pain so hidden. I see you still before your easel. Beautiful brush strokes from within. Your memory lives within us. With deep respect, love and compassion. May

you find peace in the oneness of all beings. Great Spirit,
bless us all.

I began to think I would never get to the bottom of
that box as I absorbed all the sentiments that had once so
described Chris and spoke of my experience.

Wherever a beautiful soul has been, love's never lost; love
never ends; sorrow runs deep, but love runs deeper; a leaf
is released from the arms of a tree to glide through the air,
now totally free; a journey to make, a goodbye to us all, a
beautiful brilliance we'll always recall.

One by one, I dropped the words like falling leaves
into the recycle bin that I had set by my chair for that
purpose. When I finally reached the bottom of the box,
there sat the plastic bag that had once held Chris' ashes,
folded neatly and reverently. My momentum carried me
now and I discarded it easily, wondering why I had held on
to it in the first place. I set aside a few photographs of the
anniversary rafting trip. I would keep those.

Then, I opened the little flyer that we had designed for Chris' Celebration of Life. I was struck by Chris' own words that we had chosen as a memorial to be printed on that page. He had written them a while back as a tribute to one of his paintings called *Lighthouse*.

"Very few of us can say that life is easy. My coastline is as ragged as yours. But for me, there has always been a lighthouse... those who love me or simply appreciate my art."

The dismantling was complete. With Santana cuddled on my lap, I offered up a prayer of thanks. Thanks to God for giving me the strength to get through this and for helping me through my journey, and for all the blessings that I now have in my life—the people and the divine messages that have been the lighthouse and guided me in my journey from being lost and adrift at sea, to finding the shore again.

The candle that I had lit hours before was still burning. I blew it out. With a smile and while watching the smoke rise, I imagined the white wisps as a vehicle carrying the magnificent energy of Chris into the heavens and releasing him forever. Finally, I blow him a kiss.

For all the times I had tried to let go of Chris, over the years, it had been a slow but steady process. That day, on April 10, 2012, I truly moved on. So did Chris—in gratitude, in prayer and in love. If our story in some small way can help you or someone you love to find freedom and healing, then Chris and I have accomplished our purpose together in this life.

Scientists have proven that our thoughts and feelings can change the energy around us. And many prophets, scholars and experts predict that we are living in the last days of our world as we now know it. Imagine if each of us purposefully embraced Chris' gift of internal peace. Imagine if in this moment, we choose to live our lives true to our soul's purpose; if right now we each begin to honor our divine purpose and refuse to let anyone or anything stifle who we were meant to be. At whatever point we make these decisions of the heart, our day-to-day experience is certain to transform into a more peaceful reality for each and every one of us. Then, as a result, together we can change the energy of our world.

This book began with a thought, and grew into a desire for personal healing and then into a deeper desire to extend that healing to help others to heal and grow. So in honor of Christopher Lyle Cardin, his memory, his art and his life, please accept this sincere and humble offering of—*Peace, My Final Gift*.

If there is any personal advice that I can offer in complete humility it is this—whenever you feel that life is too difficult to bear, go inward. Tap into the spirit of God that lies within you. That spirit is your only true strength. And whether this day is filled with immense joy or deep heartache, remember—we must live,

Just this day—No more.

Mary L. Cardin

A Message from the Author

The youngest of ten children, I was raised in a devout Mennonite family in central Pennsylvania. After marrying my artist husband, I left behind the loving but rigid restraints of my childhood and youth and moved to Atlanta, Georgia where I lived for most of my adult life. I was a working wife for many years, pursuing a career with a small but vital company that pioneered psychological recovery for persons suffering in the immediate aftermath of traumatic experiences.

Ironically, I owe the inspiration for my memoir to a number of devastating and life-changing events that occurred in my own life—experiences which became even more traumatic by occurring within a very short span of time.

This memoir, my first writing, was given birth in a two-year journal kept while in the midst of my pain and as I looked inward and as I searched for my own recovery and healing. The credibility of my writing is in its non-fiction reality. I lived these traumatic events and I learned how to survive them. I am now sharing these experiences and the very personal and powerful secrets of my own successful healing.

From my early childhood, I had dreamed of one day living somewhere in America's Southwest. In 2007, I fulfilled that dream by moving, with my little dog, across the country to Durango, Colorado. There I have begun a new life and a new career as owner of a successful in-home, non-medical senior care business called Shining Star Caregivers. The name was inspired by my late husband, Chris, who always called me his shining star.

Thank you for taking the time to read my story. I truly hope it has helped you and blessed you in some way and that you can pass those gifts on to others.

Acknowledgements

Friends

Not only from Durango, but from all across the country. I am truly blessed to have a network of friends, both old and new, that I can call true friends who accept, support, encourage and love me for me. I choose not to name them here because I don't want to exclude anyone - you know who you are.

Families

I received so much love, support, and generosity from members of both my family and Chris' family, for which I will be eternally grateful. One never knows the level of support you will receive until something like this happens. Thank you all.

My nieces and nephews

What an amazing bunch! I want to acknowledge the ones that helped pay for my individual therapy sessions: Tonya, Nell, Julie, Jennifer, Lisa, Michelle, Tracy, Troy, Jeremy, Jeff H. and Jeff S. It sounds trite, but your generosity really came through for me in my darkest hour, and I thank each and every one of you. I love all my nieces and nephews, and am honored to be your Auntie Mare.

Mary Jo

My sister-in-law, but a sister in the truest sense of the word. You walked with me through the valley of darkness to find your brother, Christopher Lyle, and you continue to walk beside me in our mutual healing journey. Thank you for your unconditional love and devotion. I love you and will forever be your sister.

Nancy and Carl

I am so amazed at the depth of love, support and generosity from you two wonderful people. Not only are you my family, but you are the best friends that anyone could ever ask for. I honestly believe that we are born into the family that will meet our needs to survive life's experiences and to follow our life's purpose. Part of my survival was because of your loving spirits. How does one adequately say thank you for that gift? I hope you know and I hope that I can someday return the same level of love to you that you have given me.

Sändra

Meeting you confirms my belief that timing is everything.
You came to me after I had asked for the right editor—
someone professional *and* spiritual. And as it often goes, I
received much more than I asked for. I have been blessed
by you both personally and professionally and will be
eternally grateful that you were the one to give life to my
writing. In the beginning, my editor. Now, my friend.

And of course, Chris

I miss you greatly but honor your decision to leave this
world when you did. I will always treasure the hidden gifts
that your death has given me—the love and friendship of
your sister, the deep love I still feel from you now, and the
opportunity to go inward to find *me* and the ability to find
the strength and courage to live. I am so blessed to have
had you in my life for 30 plus years and am honored to
continue your art legacy for you. As long as I live, you will
live.

Mary L. Cardin

Peace, My Final Gift

Mary L. Cardin

Made in the USA
Charleston, SC
27 June 2012